Nothing Remains the Same

Nothing Remains the Same
Jermantown, Legato, Pender, and Waples Mill during the 1920s and 1930s in Fairfax County, Virginia

Vincent D. Sutphin

History4All, Inc.
Fairfax, Virginia

Nothing Remains the Same:
Jermantown, Legato, Pender, and Waples Mill
during the 1920s and 1930s in Fairfax County, Virginia

© 2008 by Vincent D. Sutphin

Published by History4All, Inc.
Post Office Box 1126
Fairfax, Virginia 22038
history4all-books@live.net

ISBN 978-1-934285-08-4
Library of Congress Control Number: 2008942301

Printed in the United States of America
First Edition
First Printing, April 2009
Second Printing, May 2009

All Rights Reserved. No part of this book may be reproduced in any manner whatsoever without prior written permission from the publisher except in the cases of brief quotations used for the purpose of critical reviews or in scholarly manuscripts.

Maps by Vincent D. Sutphin, Fairfax, Virginia
Editing by Susan Hellman, Herndon, Virginia
Compositing and Manufacturing by Baldersons Inc., Chantilly, Virginia
Indexes by Becky Hornyak, Dumfries, Virginia

Inside cover photographs are of the author's house. *Taken by Lee Hubbard, April 2009*

This Book is Dedicated in Memory of

Linda Ann Sutphin Scott 1945-2007
(Daughter of Vincent D. Sutphin)

Dr. James E. Swart 1946-1981
(Son of John F. Swart, Jr.)

Robert A. Swart 1960-1983
(Son of Mr. and Mrs. Asa A. Swart)

This daughter and sons are from families who represent a large portion of the owners and developers of the area covered by my book.

Table of Contents

Preface   1

Jermantown Map   2

Legato Map   3

Pender Map   4

Waples Mill Map   5

    Chapter 1   The Beginning   7

    Chapter 2   Old Jermantown School and Hall   15

    Chapter 3   The Civil War Hospital   21

    Chapter 4   Jermantown North   35

    Chapter 5   Jermantown West   45

    Chapter 6   Milestone 16–Difficult Run   63

    Chapter 7   Jermantown Area–North Side of Warrenton Pike   69

    Chapter 8   Jermantown Area–South Side of Warrenton Pike   77

    Chapter 9   The Church and School at Pender   91

    Chapter 10   Pender   111

    Chapter 11   Legato–South Side of Warrenton Pike   125

    Chapter 12   Legato–North Side of Warrenton Pike   143

    Chapter 13   Waples Mill Community   155

    Chapter 14   Waples Mill Area   169

    Chapter 15   Oakton Road   183

About the Author   191

Acknowledgements   196

Name Index   197

Subject Index   203

Property Index   206

Preface

My name is Vincent D. Sutphin. I was born in what is now the City of Fairfax, Virginia, in November 1917. My parents were Ernest J. Sutphin and Jobie Twombly Sutphin. During November 1924, my family moved from Fairfax to Jermantown onto a 28-acre farm purchased from my grandmother, Mary Beach Twombly. To me, a boy of six, this was the true beginning of a love for the open space and these recollections I am about to pass on before it becomes too late. *Nothing Remains the Same* covers the Jermantown, former Pender, Legato,[1] and Waples Mill[2] neighborhoods (and some of the Vale area) of Fairfax County as they were during the 1920s and 1930s and no longer are.

During that time period, the area began to grow. The first development I recall was the construction of a tourist camp. This camp consisted of some twelve to fifteen one-room, frame cabins. Each cabin had a bed, several chairs, a King wood heater stove, and was lighted with a single electric bulb in the center of the room. Toilet facilities with showers, as well as additional cabins, were located in the center of the camp along a graveled driveway. The owner's Cape Cod frame home was also located along this semi-circle driveway with entrances along Route 236. The owner, Mr. Stoner, also ran a small lunchroom with a counter and booths, and he named the operation

---

[1] Pronounced Le-gate-oh, with accent on second syllable. It is not Le-got-oh, a common mispronunciation.
[2] Rhymes with "maples."

Kamp Washington. After several years, two gas stations, a garage, another lunchroom (the Black Lantern Inn), and a tearoom had been established at the Route 236–50 and Route 29 intersection.

The property descriptions contained within this book are drawn from my memory, personal notes, interviews, and photographs taken by me and others over the years. I have provided you, the reader, with four maps to orient you to the properties' locations within each of the neighborhoods. There also is a separate index for finding properties by their numbers, which, because I did this research over a period of ten years, sometimes jump around. There are over 150 properties listed and 200 family surnames mentioned.

Jermantown Map

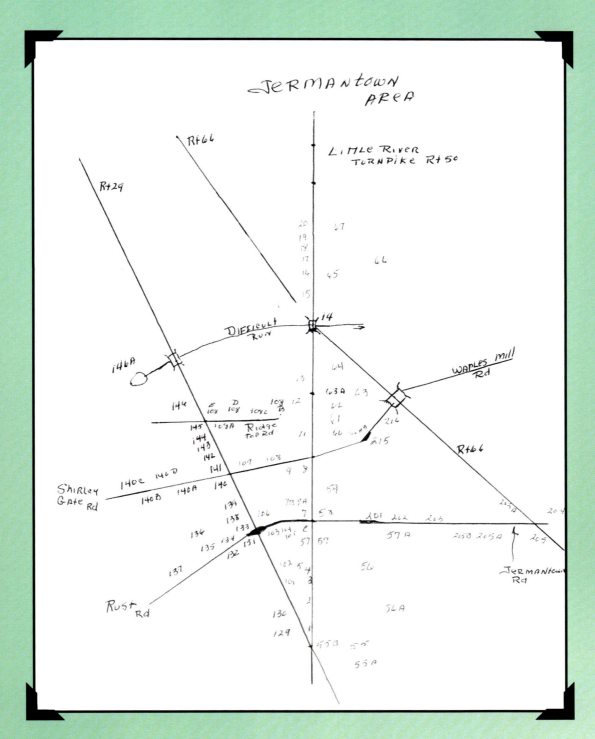

Legato Map

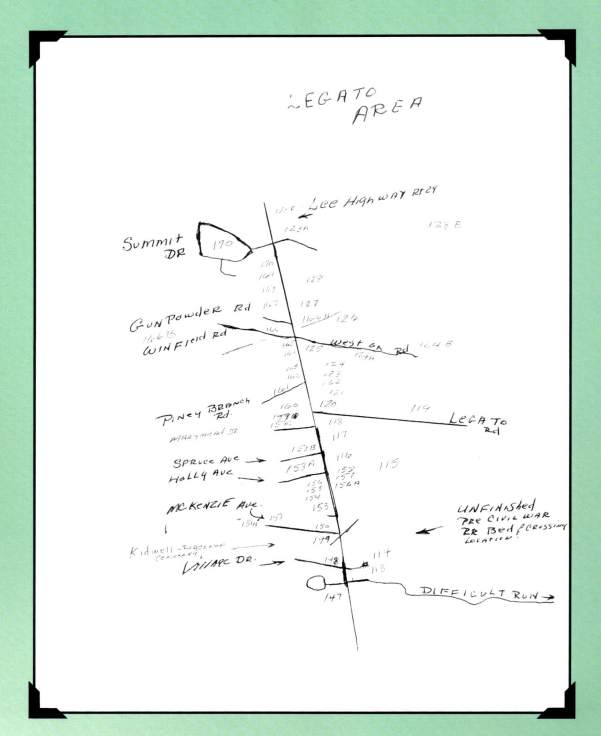

Pender Map

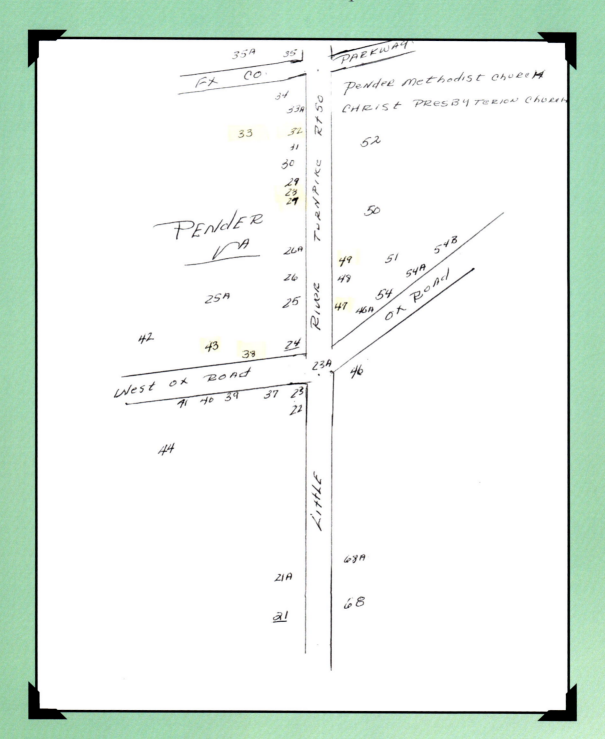

Nothing Remains the Same

Waples Mill Map

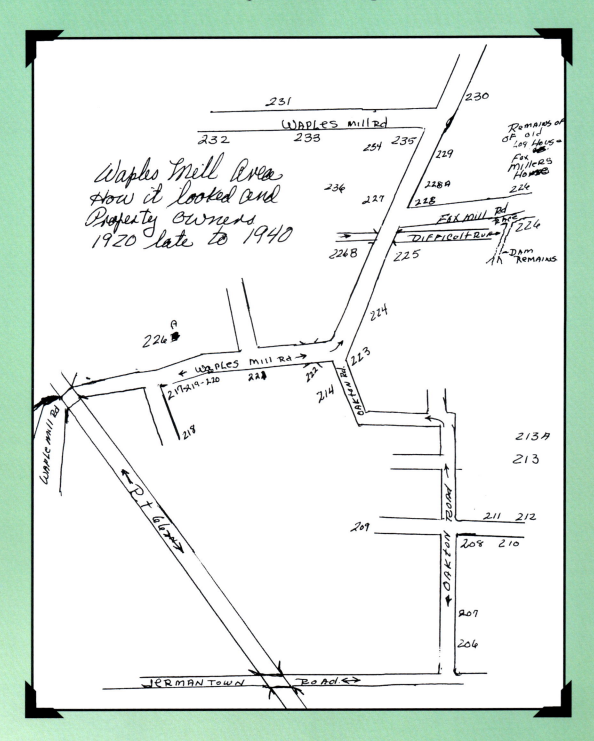

Chapter 1

The Beginning

Property 1

The first property to be reviewed by me was located at the Routes 50-29-211-236 intersection. The house faced east and was a two-story, frame construction. The family living in the house, when I started school in 1925, was the Cooks. At that time the property must have contained from 5 to 10 acres. This property was later acquired by two ladies who operated The Black Lantern Inn. After World War II the property was developed as commercial property as it is today.

Property 2

Jermantown Cemetery. This land was purchased by former slaves and freed blacks following the Civil War, I was told by older people when I was a small child. During the 1930s on a clear fall or winter day, the top of the Washington Monument was visible from that location. The cemetery is now operated by the City of Fairfax.

Property 3

This property was owned by the Smith Jerman family. The family home was a large frame two-story house with a front porch. The Jerman family was well established in the Jermantown area. Mr. Smith Jerman worked as a teamster and during the late 1890s drove for Steven P. Twombly. During the late 1920s Mr. Jerman sold this property and moved to The Plains, Virginia, in Fauquier County. There Mr. Jerman opened a general store and butcher shop. The old home location is now owned by Ted Britt Ford.

Property 4

The owners of this property were Louis and Mary V. Sisson Dindlebeck. This property is now occupied by Dominion Power Company. The Dindlebeck family, as I knew them, consisted of Clayton, Grace, Mamie, and Robert. Mamie married Ralph Waple and members of both families lived on the property until after World War II. Following World War II the property may have passed through several owners before it was developed by Dominion Power Company.

Property 5

This property was owned by the Scott family. This was a small lot with an outlet to Route 50. There was a small house on the property. It is now a part of Ted Britt Ford.

Property 6

The property at the intersection of Route 50 and Jermantown Road was owned by William Harrison before the Civil War. I believe Mr. Harrison owned all four corners. His daughter, Florence Harrison, married John H. Swart after the Civil War. On the southeast corner of this intersection, the Swart family erected a large two-story house with a front porch. The house became the main family dwelling, and members were Maggie, John F., Stacy, Florence, and Gwendolyn. The 1900 census indicates that William Harrison, father-in-law, lived with the Swart family. The four corners of this intersection today are occupied by two banks, a Shell gas station and the Giant food store.

1.1 Property 6, the John H. Swart house, now the site of a United Bank.
Photograph by John Swart

1.2 Property 6, Route 50 looking west at Jermantown Road, formerly John H. Swart property.

1.3 Property 6, Jermantown Road/Route 50 interchange looking south, formerly John H. Swart property.

CHAPTER 1 *The Beginning*

1.4   Property 6, Route 50 west at Jermantown Road.

1.5   Property 6, Route 50 west at Jermantown Road today.

Nothing Remains the Same

Property 7

Our property discussion continues to the southwest corner of Jermantown Road and Route 50. The size of this property is unknown, but there must have been several acres, as it contained a large garden spot and a large two-story frame house, which was owned by the Stacy and Halley Swart family, including their two sons, Sterling and Frank Daniel. Also on this lot was a two- story building with a large assembly hall on the second floor. Water for the three Swart homes, as well as a dairy operation, was supplied by a dug well with an automatic deep well pump. The property today is occupied by a Shell gasoline station.

Property 7A

South on Jermantown Road on the west side during the 1930s, stood an old log house, which was there before the Civil War. This was the former home of William Harrison, who claimed to have owned all four corners of this intersection before the Civil War. William Harrison's only known daughter, Florence, married John H. Swart. This property today may be occupied by a fast-food restaurant.

Property 7B

The house that stood on this property was built after World War II ended and was owned by John F. Swart. This property is now occupied by Fairfax Court Center, a shopping area.

To prevent confusion, we move to the north side of the Little River Turnpike and pick up Jermantown Road moving north on both west and east sides for approximately one mile to its intersection with Oakton Road.

Property 201

The first property on the west side of Jermantown Road north of Frank Swart's property was owned by the Hailman family. This property may have had from 5 to 10 wooded acres and contained a frame, two-story house. This property is now covered with apartments and is fully developed.

CHAPTER 1   *The Beginning*

Property 202

This property belonged to an old German immigrant by the name of Oscar Christeller. The house on the property was two-story, unpainted, and unkempt. The property was 10 to 15 wooded and overgrown acres. The owner had emigrated from Germany after World War I. During 1938 I was working for my brother Aubrey in the old Down's store at Jermantown. Adolph Hitler was coming to full power in Germany and making his move to annex Czechoslovakia and make the agreement with the British Prime Minister Neville Chamberlain. All this news was on the radio. I was very interested because of the threat of war and I was of the proper age for the draft if the United States became involved. Mr. Christeller was also interested. He would appear to listen to Hitler and his raving, and he would interpret some of the speeches to me. As he was an old man, I would listen but never agree. As well as my memory serves me I think he passed away before World War II. Today this property is occupied by apartments and by Providence Elementary School.

Property 203

The next property contained a small house, which was occupied by a black lady by the name of Nancy Bernaugh until her death. This property was then sold, and occupied by Jim Moore and his wife, Lillian S. Moore. The Moores sold this property after World War II and the house was torn down and larger homes built on the property.

Property 203A

One other property occupied the area where Route 66 crosses under Jermantown Road, but I fail to come up with the names of the property owners.

Property 204

The house that stood on the corner of Oakton Road and Jermantown Road was owned by the Smith family. One son, Albert, was an old Oakton High School graduate in the class of 1935.

Property 205

The next property was owned by the Millan family with a large frame house facing Chain Bridge Road (Route 123). During World War II, the property was sold and developed as Fairfax Acres subdivision.

Property 205A

The next property was on the east side of Jermantown Road and had a very nice looking, two-story painted house and several well-kept outbuildings. This property was owned by the Dirbershier family. I do not know Mr. Dirbershier's occupation, the size of the property, or any details. This property was acquired by Fairfax County and is now occupied by a garage and potter's field (cemetery).

Property 205B

Located on the east side of Jermantown Road, just off Route 50, are a bank, a hotel, Sidney Lanier School, a day school and nursery, a church, and several homes. All of this property was vacant before World War II and has now been developed. The bank property, 7-11 store, and some of the school property were owned by the Swart family.

Chapter 2

Old Jermantown School and Hall

Property 8

The land for the old Jermantown school building was donated to Fairfax County by Stephen P. and Mary B. Twombly, my grandparents. Former known teachers at this school, which closed prior to 1925, were Robert Allison, later sheriff of Fairfax County; Leo Haines, later a DC lawyer; and Miss Lillian Millan. This building was sold after its closing, and it was purchased by Mr. George Hall. It was later remodeled and turned into a dwelling. Mr. Hall rented this property for a number of years including the Sisson Family, after which it was sold and torn down. The property is now occupied by a small shopping area with several stores.

2.1 Property 8, the Jermantown School, closed in 1930 and remodeled as a dwelling with front and side porches added. Sam Sisson family reunion in progress.
Courtesy of members of the Sam Sisson family

Property 9

The old Jermantown Hall was a large frame, two-story, weatherboard and unpainted structure with an east side entrance. I do not remember a front entrance. The roof rose some 6 to 8 feet over the second story side walls. The first and second story had a pine tongue-and-groove floor and the walls were unfinished. The front end of the building contained two windows, and the east and west sides each had at least two windows. On the north end, the first and second floor contained a small stage, which rose approximately 18 inches above the floor, as well as I remember. The first and second floor ceilings were unfinished. I am also unable to remember any chimney for heating arrangements. From the side entrance on the first floor, a stairway led to the second story level. This building was used for religious services and community affairs. The land this building was built on was donated by the Swart family. The Haines family, as well as other local families in the Jermantown community, was also involved in the general operations. How money for the construction of this large building was obtained was never made clear to me. This building was allowed to deteriorate after the Pender Methodist Church was established in 1907. This building site is no longer visible, as the new Waples Mill Road between Route 50 and Route 29 covers its former location. With the help of the yearbook for the Fiftieth Golden Anniversary of the Pender Methodist Church, 1907-1957, I have come up with an interpretation of religion and entertainment at old Jermantown from 1860 to 1900.

Religion at Jermantown: Fairfax Circuit

Reverend William Gwynn Coe, DD, preacher at Fairfax Methodist Church, 1859-1861, also preached at Jermantown, which was also known as Wells Mission. On February 21, 1860, he preached at the funeral of Mrs. Wells, a hundred-year-old lady, at Jermantown. This was before the circuit was started. During 1900, Mr. F.M. Allder was appointed Superintendent of Sunday School for Wells Mission at Jermantown, at the request of Mr. M.G. Jerman. In 1880 Mr. M.G. Jerman, Recording Steward of the Fairfax Circuit, began conducting Sunday School at Millan School House near Jermantown, two miles from Fairfax and two miles from Pender. Dr. J.H. Dalaney, a dentist and preacher, was a once-a-month preacher at what was known as Wells Mission. In 1881 the Reverend Collins Denny, Pastor of Fairfax Circuit, conducted a Bush Meeting at Wells Mission. This lasted three days. All this information was obtained from Pender Methodist Church history booklet. The church was organized in 1903.

Jermantown Wells Mission:

Methodist Church

In 1907 Mr. F.M. Allder, who served at Wells Mission as Superintendent of Sunday School, was appointed Superintendent of Pender Methodist Church and Sunday School. The Pender Sunday School gradually absorbed the Wells Mission Sunday School. The Pender Methodist Church History was printed by the Virginia Press of Fairfax, Virginia, for the church's Fiftieth Golden Anniversary, 1907-1957, and was celebrated June 9, 1957. The historical sketch was written by Melvin Lee Steadman, Jr.

Black Families in the Area

The black men and women who lived in the Jermantown area are listed below. Those marked with an asterisk, I have been told, were former slaves and the owners are unknown.

Lucy Jackson
*Cindy Lucas
John Jackson (Lucy's husband who worked for George Beach.)
Washington Payne (Born free. Worked for George Beach.)
*Becky Ashton (Worked for S.P. Twombly.)
Fred Ashton (Son of Becky.)
Winfree Runner   (Unknown.)
Ben Runner   (Unknown.)
*Buck Horton (Unknown. Lived in Fairfax.)
Nancy Bernaugh (Unknown. Lived on Jermantown Road at the
     Route 66 overpass.)
Charity Payne (Born free. Washington Payne's wife.)
Charley Payne (Son of Washington and Charity Payne.)
Jake Colbert (Lived at Route 29 and Jermantown Road, east
     corner.)
Clarence Colbert (Son of Jake. Lived at same location.)
Charlie Scott and wife (Lived midway between Route 29 and
     Route 50 on Jermantown Road.)

J. Clarke and wife, Margaret, a sister of Cindy Lucas (This couple's home was on the north side of Route 50 east of the Jermantown/Route 50 interchange approximately 1,000 feet.)

A. Waley and wife (On south side of Route 50 across the highway from J. Clarke and his wife.)

Dick Chambers and wife (South side of Route 50 approximately 400 feet east of the A. Waley house set back from the highway approximately 400 feet.)

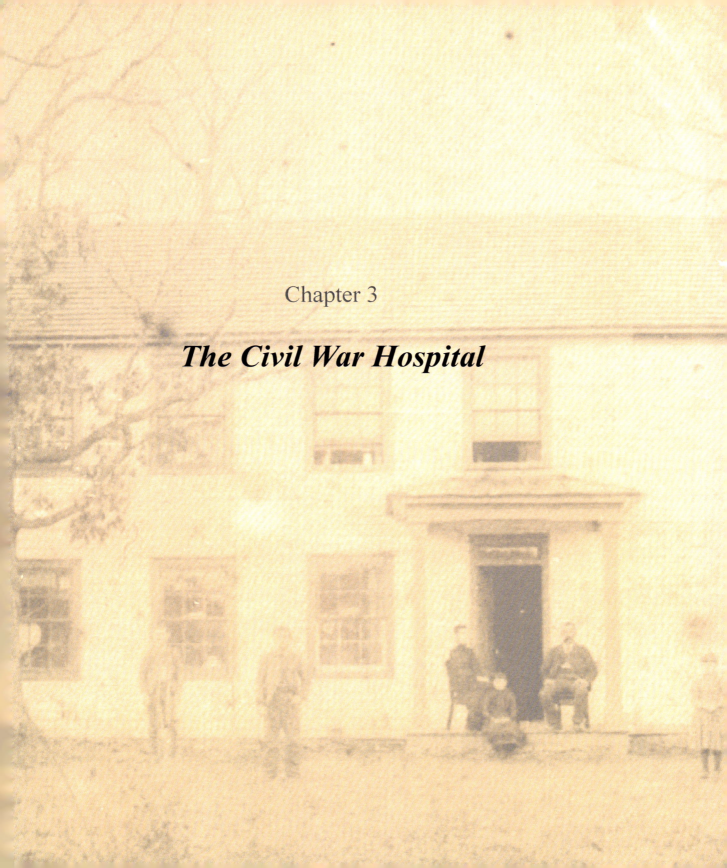

Chapter 3

The Civil War Hospital

3.1 Stephen P. Twombly, Civil War veteran, 1st Maine Cavalry.
Courtesy of Twombly/Sutphin family collection

3.2 Mary E. Twombly.
Courtesy of Twombly/Sutphin family collection

Property 11

The Stephen P. and Mary Beach Twombly property contained approximately 13 acres. It was a part of the former Tapley Worster property. This property was acquired from George and Martha Worster Beach, Mrs. Twombly's brother and his wife. The house was a large eight-room, two-story L-shaped, frame and weatherboard home. Outbuildings consisted of a milk and dairy house with a basement, a carriage house, a large horse and cow barn, and a hand-dug well with a well house. This well contained hard water, which was almost impossible to drink or use for domestic purposes. Stephen P. Twombly operated a general store at this location, as well as a huckster business. Stephen Twombly also operated several other general stores besides the Jermantown store. These were located at Gainesville, Buckland, and

CHAPTER 3 *The Civil War Hospital*

3.3 Property 11, the S.P. Twombly home in 1890s. Photograph taken by traveling photographer of (left to right) Sam Robey, George Twombly, Stanley Twombly, Jobie Twombly, Mary Beach Twombly, Stephen Twombly, Nellie Twombly, and Mamie Twombly. *Courtesy of V.D. Sutphin collection*

Orleans, Virginia. This business required the use of two- and three-horse wagon teams. They traveled between the stores delivering merchandise to be sold and to pick up merchandise traded at the stores. This would include eggs, poultry, all kinds of apples and peaches in season, as well as livestock. Two wagon teams were kept on the road at all times. One to pick up the produce, and the other to deliver the produce to the Washington market. Additional side trips, when required, would be made to Amissville, Gaines Cross Roads, Ben Venue, View Town, and Sperryville, Virginia. Teamsters who drove the teams were Tom Lee, Smith Jerman, Hezekiah Jerman, Harry Graham, Deskin Monroe, and George Twombly, Stephen's son. Stephen's other son, Stanley Twombly, operated stores at Gainesville and Buckland, Virginia. Pat Driscoll, a drover, would occasionally stop with his crew at the Jermantown store. His crew was made up of six to eight boys who kept herds of cattle, hogs, turkeys, and sheep in line and kept them moving on their way to the Washington or Alexandria markets. Another interesting fact about the Twombly property was the location of a Civil War Hospital on the north corner. The dead from this hospital were buried on another property

3.4 Property 11, the site of the S.P. Twombly home today. Note that the top of the tree in this photograph is depicted behind the Twombly home, on the right, in Figure 3.3.

3.5 Property 11, the site of the S.P. Twombly home today, 11350 Random Hills Road.

CHAPTER 3   *The Civil War Hospital*

located on the south side of the Twombly property. These remains were removed by a Mr. James W. Taylor, a Fairfax undertaker, around 1900. This information was obtained by me from my uncle, George P. Twombly. This may have been the location of the Confederate Camp Pettus Regional Hospital at Jermantown, Virginia, as mentioned on page 80 in the book *Brothers and Cousins, Confederate Soldiers and Sailors of Fairfax County* compiled by William Page Johnson II.

Stephen P. Twombly died in 1906 and is buried in the Fairfax Cemetery. This brought an end to the huckster business. The Twombly children were Mamie, who married Norman Stewart; George, who married Bessie Ball; Stanley M., who married Anna Cook; Nellie, who married Richard H. Downs; and Jobie, who married Ernest J. Sutphin. The property is now covered by large buildings and a parking lot. Stephen P. Twombly was born in Yarmouth, Maine in 1841, and died in 1906 in Fairfax, Virginia. He enrolled in the 1st Maine Cavalry at Augusta, Maine, on November 7, 1861, for a period of three years. He was discharged from service November 28, 1864, at Washington, DC, having served three years and 21 days. Prisoner of War records indicate that he was taken prisoner on October 13/14, 1863, at Thornburgh Gap, Virginia, and sent to Richmond, Virginia, on October 23, 1863. From prison at Richmond, he was transferred to Andersonville, Georgia. Prisoner of War camp records are conflicting, as a statement for pension made by Twombly in 1881 states he was sent from Danville prison to Andersonville, Georgia. Prisoner of War records show that his transfer was made on March 1, 1864. During the trip from Richmond or Danville, Virginia, in April of 1864, he jumped from the railroad car and was shot, but made good his escape and rejoined the Federal Army at New Bern, North Carolina. After rejoining the army at New Bern, North Carolina, he was sent to a Camp Stephen near Washington DC, and later discharged or mustered out of the army. On November 3, 1870, he married my grandmother, Mary E. Beach. This marriage was performed in Fairfax County by George H. William and is recorded on the Registrar of Marriages of this county.

3.6 Property 12, the George and Martha W. Beach home, part of the old Worster farm, on the south side of Route 50.

3.7 Property 12 on left, Difficult Run Hill. The Beach farm is on the left and the Swart farm is on the right. The Swart farm, Property 64, is discussed in Chapter 6.

CHAPTER 3 *The Civil War Hospital*

3.8   Property 12, the Beach farm in October 1959.

3.9   Property 12, the Beach farm today.

Property 12

George and Martha W. Beach were the owners of the next property. This consisted of all the remaining Tapley Worster property, which ran along the south side of Little River Turnpike from the Twombly property line to about 1,000 feet west of Difficult Run. This property contained 90 acres, more or less. George Beach operated a dairy and general farm with a small orchard. Each day the milk produced was hauled to the Washington market. Two workers on the farm were John Jackson and Washington Payne. After the dairy operation was closed down, due to Mr. Beach's age, the farm was leased to various individuals. The Beachs were a well-respected couple. Their farm was a neighborhood showplace and ran along the south side of Little River Turnpike for over a mile. There was a 30-acre small farm on the north side of the turnpike at Milestone 16, the west boundary or property line. The Beach children were a son, Forrest, and a daughter, Martha. All members of the Beach family are interred at Fairfax Cemetery. The property is now included in Random Hills subdivision and the Route 50/Route 66 interchange.

3.10 Property 13, the Tapley Worster dwelling, south side of Route 50. The Difficult Run Hill field was occupied by Ohio troops during the Battle of Ox Hill. Tapley Worster was a veteran of the War of 1812, according to his tombstone in Fairfax Cemetery. His remains were relocated there from the family burying grounds in 1960, during the construction of the Route 50/Route 66 interchange. This house was remodeled in 1940.

CHAPTER 3 *The Civil War Hospital*

3.11 Property 13, the Tapley Worster dwelling, kitchen, and slave quarters. This section was not rebuilt during the 1940 renovations. Before the Civil War, this was a farm of approximately 200 acres. It also operated as a drovers' rest and stagecoach stop.

3.12 Property 13, old kitchen and slave quarters to the Tapley Worster main house. All were removed during the construction of the Route 50/Route 66 interchange.

Nothing Remains the Same

Property 13

The Tapley Worster home and property was located at the top of Difficult Run Hill. This house, with a large barn and loft, was a drovers' overnight stop both before and after the Civil War. Both male and female slaves were used in this type of operation. Meals and lodging were available to the drovers and their crews. The drovers carried feed for their herd and obtained water from the creeks they had passed over on the road. The Worster house was a large two-story, frame building with two front entrances. The roof was of medium height. The house had a half basement under the east end. The back section contained the kitchen with a fireplace and cooking facilities. Besides the kitchen, there were two other rooms with loft facilities for sleeping. These rooms must have been assigned to the several slaves who worked the farm and provided the labor to run the drover business for the Worster family. This is believed to be the case, as I have never heard anyone mention separate slave quarters or cabins. Water for this operation was obtained from a ninety foot, hand-dug well, which was lined with flint rock. Mr. Jim Seaton cleaned this well in 1935 with the help of my father. This well information was obtained by me at that time. The Worster family was interred on the property with their slaves. During the construction of the Route 50/Route 66 interchange, those interred there were moved to Herndon and Fairfax cemeteries.

3.13 Property 14, the single arch bridge on Little River Turnpike, Route 50, over Difficult Run. This bridge was not destroyed during the Civil War. Construction date unknown.

CHAPTER 3   *The Civil War Hospital*

3.14 Property 14, Difficult Run Hill looking east from the bridge. The Swart farm, Property 64, is on the left and the Beach farm, Property 12, is on the right.

Property 14

The location of the old fieldstone arch bridge over Difficult Run was on Little River Turnpike. At the west end of the bridge, the elevation of the road dropped approximately four feet with a curve to the left. During inclement weather such as rain and snow, this arrangement caused many automobile and truck accidents. The old bridge and road remained in use until the Route 50/Route 66 interchange was completed. My efforts to save the old arch bridge were not successful and it was demolished.

Property 15

The Robert Snapp/Sherwood home consisted of 20 or more acres and was primarily operated as a truck farm with the sale of strawberries, rhubarb, sugar corn, beans, and other garden products. Mr. Snapp also worked as a carpenter. Mr. Snapp married Elizabeth E. Sherwood and had two sons, James B. and Louis M. His sisters-in-law, who also lived at this location, were Margaret F. Sherwood and Laura F. Sherwood. Most of this property is included in the Route 50/Route 66 interchange.

3.15 Property 16, the Luther Randolph Sherwood homeplace, built 1909.
Courtesy of his granddaughter, Mrs. Shirley Vanvleet

3.16 Property 16, the Luther Randolph Sherwood farm.
Courtesy of Mrs. Shirley Vanvleet

Property 16

The Luther Sherwood and Ethel Haines Sherwood home contained 40 acres, more or less. Mr. Sherwood operated a small orchard and sold apples, grapes, and other farm products from a roadside stand. He also built and sold houses, and was employed by the government in Washington. The property was split between the Sherwoods' three children, (Maxwell C., Pauline, and Quentin) after Mr. Sherwood's death during World War II. Mrs. Ethel Haines Sherwood preceded him in death some years before. Both are interred in Fairfax Cemetery. All of this property is now included in the Route 50/Route 66 interchange.

Property 16A

Location of the Quentin and Ruth Sherwood home.

Property 17

Location of the Pauline and Edward X. Miller home.

Property 18

Location of Claude and Lillian Rollins Twombly home built during the late 1930s on the George and Bessie Twombly property. All of this property is now included in the Route 50/Route 66 interchange.

Property 19

Location of George and Bessie Ball Twombly property consisting of 30 acres, more or less. The property was a gift from his parents, Stephen and Mary Twombly. It was then passed on to his three children: Claude, Eunice, and Louise Twombly. The Twombly daughters graduated from the old Oakton High School—Eunice, class of 1924, and Louise, class of 1929. All of this property is now included in Fair Oaks Shopping Center on the Route 50/Route 66 interchange.

Property 20

Location of Stanley M. and Annie Cook Twombly property, which consisted of 30 acres, more or less. This property was a gift from his parents, Stephen and Mary Twombly. The Stanley Twombly family sold this property and moved to Vienna, Virginia. The property then changed hands several times before it was included in the Fair Oaks Shopping Center and Route 50/Route 66 interchange.

This will end what is considered the Jermantown area on the south side of Little River Turnpike.

Chapter 4

Jermantown North

Property 55

The first property in this area, during the 1920s to the 1950s, was a good-size farm owned by Mr. F.W. Huddleston, who had previously been the Treasurer of Fairfax County. The farm contained 145 acres and covered an area from the old Fairfax town limits west along Route 50 about one-half mile, and north to the property of the old Fairfax Fair Grounds, and in the eastern direction into the town of Fairfax. This included the old Rumsey property. Mr. Huddleston employed people to operate this as a dairy farm for him. Some of the families so employed were Erskine, Higgdon, Guy Poland, John Sutphin, Durley Sutphin, and George Anderson.

Property 55A

The house located on this property was a two-story, frame home. Other buildings included a barn and a shed for the dairy machines. The sheds were of frame construction and painted red. At the highway entrance to the farm was the Milestone 15.

Property 55B

These milestones were placed every mile from Alexandria to Aldie when Little River Turnpike was built during colonial times. The stones disappeared after 1945 during the Route 50 rebuilding. F.W. Huddleston also owned Fairview Farms in the Chantilly area containing 1,000 acres. This farm was also operated as a dairy farm under a similar setup. The milk produced by both farms was combined and hauled to Washington each day on a truck owned by Mr. Huddleston. Both farms are now covered with housing and commercial development. During the 1920s, Mr. F.W. Huddleston employed Mr. Erskine to manage the Kamp Washington farm with John Sutphin to help with its operation. During the early 1930s, Mr. John Higgdon was employed with Elmer Jerman to help with the operations. During the late 1930s through the 1950s or until the farm operation was closed down, Guy Poland and his wife Helen, with George and Lucille Anderson, ran the farm operation. The Higgdon family had one son, John, and two daughters whose names I

CHAPTER 4   Jermantown North

4.1   Property 56, Fairfax County Poor House, closed in the 1930s. House had also been used as a business school, apartment house, private home, and nursing home. Front porch added 1941-1942.
Photograph by Council M. Sutphin

cannot remember. The Poland family had one daughter, Annie, who married Paul Brooks. The Andersons' children were George D., Jim, and Gary. The 1,000-acre Chantilly farm was managed by a Mr. James King, with Archie Hawes helping him and later replacing him as farm manager. There were probably others who worked on the large farm but are unknown by me.

Property 56

The Fairfax County Poor House with a potter's field (cemetery), which was some distance in the rear of the house, was located on this property. Fairfax County probably owned from 10 to 15 acres in this plot. The building was a large masonry, two-and-one-half story building at least 60 x 45 feet with a large dormer window in the roof to ventilate the attic area. My family moved from Fairfax to the Jermantown area in 1924. The county was using this facility then and continued to do so into the 1930s, when they combined operations with Prince William and Loudoun counties at Manassas, Virginia. I recall several burials in the potter's field, which included Kunter Park. After Fairfax County combined this operation with the other two counties, this property was sold.

Nothing Remains the Same   37

Property 56A

One of the renters, who leased about 5 acres on the eastern section of the property in the early 1930s, was the Virginia Department of Highways. They opened their own headquarters on Route 123 in Fairfax around 1936 or shortly thereafter. The first use of the property and house, after the county combined this type of operation with their two neighboring counties, was a welfare shelter for homeless men from the District of Columbia during the Depression. My knowledge of this is very limited and my only contact came when some of the men would shop for tobacco or toiletry items at my Uncle Henry Downs' country store. In the 1930s the large house was rented to Frank Stuart and then turned into apartments and a business school, which was operated for several years. During the 1940s, the property was purchased and remodeled as a dwelling. The last use before the house was demolished was a nursing home called Fairfax Lodge. The property was turned into commercial buildings and parking facilities.

Property 57

Two abandoned frame houses were located on Route 50. One was on the south side of Route 50, owned by A. Waley, and one on the north side, owned by J. Clarke. Both of these families were black, and following the Civil War, I have been told, made their living by selling food to drovers and herders along the highway. Over the years these small pieces of property must have been absorbed by all the wheeling and dealing in the area in real estate.

Property 57A

This property was an open field containing 5 or more acres. This lot was owned by the Swart family and used for pasture. It faced Route 50 on the front, and on the west Jermantown Road for about 1,000 feet. The property is completely developed now. It is occupied by a bank, hotel, and 7-11 store.

CHAPTER 4 *Jermantown North*

4.2 Property 58, front view of the John F. Swart home. Mr. Swart is pictured with his grandson, James E. Swart.
Photograph by John F. Swart

4.3 Property 58, the former home of John F. Swart, located at Jermantown Road and Route 50, the present location of the Giant grocery store.
Photograph by Vincent Sutphin

Property 58

On the west side of Jermantown Road, at the intersection of Little River Turnpike, was located a house and property owned by John F. Swart. This property ran approximately one-half mile along Jermantown Road, as well as several hundred feet along Route 50. This property probably contained 7 to 10 acres and is now covered with a Giant food store and several commercial buildings.

Property 58A

J. Frank Swart and family operated a dairy farm at the Jermantown Road and Route 50 intersection from the early 1920s until 1945. A few years later, Jermantown Road was hard-surfaced and traffic soon picked up in this area, which meant cattle could not be safe on the road. J. Frank Swart had two sons, John and Asa, and they were instrumental in the development of the commercial property at this intersection. They also played a large part in bringing sewer to the Route 50 area. A pumping station was installed on Difficult Run and allowed this area to develop. Their family continues to own and operate commercial properties in Fairfax County and Fairfax City. The Swart brothers and their families still live in the area.

From a Dairy Farm to Commercial Real Estate

John and Asa Swart inherited the dairy farm at Route 50 and Jermantown Road in 1950. A few years after this, it became apparent that the best use for the land used as a dairy farm for years would be commercial development. They had to get sewer to the property, so they decided to sell the northeast corner to the National Bank of Fairfax so they would bring sewer to this intersection. In the early 1960s the Town of Fairfax had become a city. They, in turn, annexed the entire intersection into the city, creating more interest in western Fairfax City. The next development attempted was the northwest corner. They entered into a lease with the Hechinger Company. In an attempt to get the entire

site into commercial zoning, they took the case to the State Supreme Court. Then the city zoned all the annexed land to a commercial category and this allowed them to move forward with development. They then encountered the County of Fairfax, because some of the land straddled the county-city line. Any additional development would require approval by both jurisdictions. In order to continue development of the properties, they became active in the Route 50-66 Association. The sole purpose of this association was to help plan the Route 50/Route 66 area and provide utilities for individual property owners. The final accomplishments of the Route 50-66 Association were a master plan, and water and sewer availability. This required the association to build sewer lines and two pumping stations, which allowed the land at Route 50 and Route 66 to be developed (this included the land at Jermantown in the county, and gave them a chance to continue the development). The first project was on the southeast of Route 50 and Waples Mill Road. They leased this ground to Montgomery Ward, who in turn sold their land lease to Simon Co., who ultimately developed the Fairfax Court Center. In order to do this, they ended up building Waples Mill Road from Route 50 to their property line on the south. Subsequent to this, they have traded the land on the west of Waples Mill Road for other properties in the county. The Swart family retains ownership of most of the original dairy farm. All of this was due to the Swart brothers' desire to preserve part of our roots to this area. They both live in Northern Virginia where they have raised their families.
[As told and written by John F. Swart, Jr.]

Property 59

The next property west was a farm containing 90 acres more or less. This farm was owned by Rose May Jerman Haines who married Robert D. Haines of Romney, West Virginia, on June 5, 1883. Before the marriage to Mr. Haines, the Jerman family, after the Civil War, operated a drovers' rest at this location. Mr. Haines farmed and also was in the huckster business selling chickens, eggs, and other produce on the Washington market. Later, from 1919 to about 1960, his son Russell continued until ill health prohibited him from doing so. This farm, during the early stages of the Civil War, in the area next to Waples Mill Road, was used as a campground of a unit from South Carolina. I have no proof of this and I am only repeating what I was told by different sources in my younger years. This property was ideal for commercial development, being level, with good drainage, having a sizeable acreage, and frontage on two roads. In a very short period of time, this has been accomplished. Some of the first money I earned was paid to me by Russell Haines to thin corn for him. As I grew older, he also employed me to help with the huckster business and the sale of produce at the old Washington Farmers' Market at 5th and K streets NW, and 5th Street and Florida Avenue NE. This was a great experience and continued during my high school years. My older brother, Council, worked regularly in this business from his graduation from high school in 1929 to the spring of 1935. The Haines family members were: Ethel, who married Luther R. Sherwood; William Garner, who married Lena F. Powell; Robert Ray, not married; Leo, who married Susan Ross; Clarence, who married Virginia Edmond; Russell, not married; Blanch, who married Lloyd Bowers; Clarice, who married Isaac Craig; and Virginia, not married.

CHAPTER 4 *Jermantown North*

4.4 Property 59, the Rosa B. Haines house. This was a large, seven-room house with front and back porches. The large farm had numerous well-built outbuildings, all used in the farming and huckstering business.
Photograph by Vincent Sutphin

Chapter 5

Jermantown West

Property 60

This 10-acre plot of land was acquired by my aunt, Nellie Twombly Downs, and her husband, Richard Henry Downs, after they returned from Maryland to take up residence with my grandmother in her home at Jermantown. Mr. Downs, for a short period of time, reopened the old store in my grandmother's house. This store had been closed by my grandmother for several years following my grandfather's death in 1906. The 10-acre plot of land acquired by the Downs' was not suitable for farming or raising garden crops. The land was rocky, hilly, and split in two ways with a wet-weather stream, and half covered in oak trees and woods. Before the Downs' purchased this property another possible owner was John J. Murry; it fits the description of property owned by him in a deed dated October 22, 1848. This deed covers one-half acre at the rear corner of the property for a gravesite for John W. Aston. In this general location, during the 1920s and 1930s, a gravesite was visibly marked with fieldstones, but with no name. This same area was also used as a picnic and community retreat. Prior to 1925, Mr. and Mrs. Downs erected a general store on their property, with several outbuildings to house chickens and hogs. During the 1930s, a large barn was erected and all buildings were painted red. Also during the 1930s, two houses were erected and the general store was enlarged. Of the original 10 acres, Mr. and Mrs. Downs sold three lots, possibly containing from ¾ to 1 acre apiece. All original buildings on this property were removed during the construction of the Route 50/Route 66 interchange. One commercial building has been erected. Ownership of the remaining properties is not clear. The old gravesite and picnic area is covered by a street intersection. Before the Downs purchased this property, the house that stood on it burned. It was owned or rented by the Mills family and the Anderson family. Mr. Mills made and sold chairs. What the Anderson family did was never made clear to me.

Waples Mill Road: The Jermantown Area

The R.H. Downs, in the summer of 1933, sold two pieces of property off the original 10 acres.

Property 60A

The first piece was sold to Miss Laura Byrns and it contained about one acre or less. On this lot, which faced Little River Turnpike (Route 50) with an east boundary on Waples

CHAPTER 5   *Jermantown West*

5.1 Property 60, the original location of the R.H. Downs Store. The store was owned and operated by R.H. Downs 1933-34; operated by A.W. Sutphin 1935-38; and operated by Austin Arborgast 1940-47. The store was relocated due to the Route 50 widening and regrading, then removed when the Route 50/Route 66 interchange was completed.
Photograph by Council Sutphin

5.2 Property 60, Aubrey W. Sutphin, leaning on his store's truck between 1935 and 1938.

Nothing Remains the Same   **47**

5.3 Property 60, Arborgast Amoco station, Waples Mill Road and Route 50. The lot today is unoccupied.
Photograph by Vincent Sutphin

5.4 Property 60, Arborgast gas station and the Henry J. Garage. These buildings were lost due to the construction of the Route 50/Route 66 interchange.

CHAPTER 5   *Jermantown West*

5.5   Property 60, general view of the Downs' property 1947-1950. Red barn, relocated R.H. Downs store operated by A. Arborgast, Gradon Cox home on the south side of Route 50, unoccupied pig house and chicken house owned by Nellie Downs, rental house, and Mrs. Downs' home.
Photograph by Vincent Sutphin

5.6   Property 60, Jermantown looking east along Route 50. Mrs. Downs' home and store, Arborgast's Henry J. Garage and Amoco Station. Haines barn and house, Property 59, discussed on pages 41-43.

5.7 Property 60, Mr. and Mrs. O.L. Berkeys' home on Waples Mill Road. Home to author and Mrs. Berkey's daughter, Ruth Wilson, from September 1945 until 1955. House built on Property 60.

5.8 Area of Property 60, the old Jermantown picnic area on the west side of Waples Mill Road near Pender Drive. Photo taken around 1900. John Frank Swart is in the third row middle, wearing a dark jacket, a hat, and a bow tie. Ethel Haines is about seven rows back, near the tree, wearing a large white hat.
Courtesy of the Twombly/Sutphin family collection

Mill Road, was built a five-room Cape Cod frame home. This house was rented and later was purchased by one of the renters, Austin and Vina Arborgast, during World War II. During the early 1930s, at the Waples Mill Road and Route 50 interchange section, the Arborgasts built a gas station. It was run by Mr. Arborgast and later rented. Mr. Arborgast then had a large building erected in which he operated an auto dealership selling Henry J (Kaiser) automobiles. When they were no longer available, he sold used automobiles and rented the gas station. These businesses continued until the two buildings and the house were absorbed in the Route 50/Route 66 interchange. The remaining property was sold. Mr. Arborgast retired and moved to Orman Beach, Florida.

Property 60B

The next piece of property sold by R.H. Downs faced Waples Mill Road on the east, and on the north where the road makes a 90-degree turn to the west. It contained about one-half acre of land, more or less. The property was sold in 1933 to R.L. Cornell and his wife. Mr. Cornell worked for the Virginia Department of Highways as a mechanic. This property covered the unmarked fieldstone grave and community picnic area. The property provided for the widening of Waples Mill Road, the 90-degree turn in the road, and an outlet for the Fairfax Ridge housing development.

The last piece of property was sold in 1942 by my aunt, Nellie T. Downs, Mr. R.H. Downs' widow, to O.L. and Macell Berkey. It contained about three quarters of an acre, more or less. This property faced Waples Mill Road on the east, the R.L. Cornell line on the north, and the Arborgast line on the south. A small frame house occupied this property, which was sold by Mrs. Berkey's daughter, Ruth W. Sutphin, on the Berkeys' deaths. The property today is occupied by commercial buildings. With the sale to the Berkey family, the Downs' property no longer had any frontage on Waples Mill Road. The construction of Route 66 through the area and the construction of its interchange with Route 50 brought about the loss of all homes in the area. When this occurred, acting for my father and mother, I was able to secure my sister's Cape

Cod frame home and had it moved to the north end of their property on Waples Mill Road. Several years prior to this, my brother Council and family built a house on Waples Mill Road, followed by my sister, Doris Dunn, and her husband, Ray Dunn. My father and mother had sold one lot on Waples Mill Road off the old farm to Charles and M. Cobb, who also built a home there. Route 66 took the Cobb property, as well as my brother Council's and his wife Lillian's property. After my parents' deaths, the Sutphin children sold the remaining property as previously mentioned, to the Georgious Company for the development of Fairfax Ridge.

Property 215

Another property that needs to be discussed in the Jermantown area was on the north side of Waples Mill Road. It was owned by a member of the Jackson family, who was black. This property probably contained from 5 to 10 acres, and it was covered with second-growth woods. Its east property line joined the Haines property, with a frontage on Waples Mill Road, and the west property line abutted the John and Lucy Jackson property. Today the property is fully developed by commercial buildings 11240 and 11242.

Property 216

The next piece of property was owned by John and Lucy Jackson. Lucy Jackson had been a slave, as well as her husband John, who had passed away before the period I am discussing. Both had worked for my uncle George and aunt Martha W. Beach, during the period following the Civil War and into the early 1900s. I was glad to know the lady. We children called her Aunt Lucy Jackson during her frequent visits to the Beach and Sutphin families' homes. The Lucy Jackson property probably contained 10 or more acres. This property was acquired by Mr. George Waple during the 1930s. He had the property split into lots and built houses, then sold each house and lot. Families who purchased them were the Ashfords, the Bramsons, the Elmer Demorys, the Goodings, the Raymond Waples, and the Schaffers, who sold to the Homes family. Today all this area is commercial with two large buildings at 11244 and

CHAPTER 5   *Jermantown West*

5.9 Property 61, the Morris Sutphin house (at far left). Built on a part of the Robety property. At far right, the Nellie T. Downs house on Property 60 (see page 46 for property description.)
Photograph by Vincent Sutphin, 1955-62

5.10 Property 61, east-end view of the Sam Robey and R.R. Robey home, which was relocated to the Jermantown area from the Pender area after the Civil War. Later, this property was acquired by Dave Goodnow.
Photograph by Vincent Sutphin, 1955-62

Nothing Remains the Same

11254.
Property 61

The next property was owned by Sam Robey and his wife. The Robeys obtained this property following the Civil War. This was a 10-acre plot of land and contained no house. When Mr. Robey purchased this property he was living near Pender, Virginia, in a log house. This house the Robeys had torn down and moved by horse and wagon to his newly purchased property and reassembled. The reassembled house contained four rooms: two downstairs and two upstairs, and were of the original log construction. There was added a shed kitchen, which was of new framed lumber. The main house contained the two downstairs and two upstairs rooms, with an open stairway along the west side of the house giving access to the upstairs rooms. To provide light to these two rooms, two dormer windows, facing south, were in the roof. Windows were also in the east and west gable end of the house. The east end of the house was occupied by a large stone and brick chimney with an opening for a furnace in the basement and a fireplace in the sitting room on the first floor. The kitchen had a brick chimney with provisions made for heating by a stove for the dining room and combination house entrance. This house also had an attractive screened back and front porch with a well pump on the back porch. The kitchen also had two entrances, one on the east and one on the west side of the house. Also, on the west side of the

5.11 Property 61, David Booker, Musette Sutphin, Vincent Sutphin, 1925, at the Robey home.
Courtesy of the Booker family

CHAPTER 5   *Jermantown West*

5.12 Property 61, a west-side view of the old Samuel Robey home on the north side of Route 50 in 1950.

house was a large white oak tree with an excellent rope swing for the use of children. Like the adjoining Downs' property, this was unsuitable for farming, as it was split by a small stream, hills, and the soil was rocky. In the rear of the property, next to Waples Mill Road, were the remains of an ice pond. This property has been explored for use of its stone for re-grading and resurfacing Little River Turnpike, but the stone was found to be too soft. When Mr. Sam Robey died and where he was interred is unknown to me.

The property passed to his son, Rodophus R. and his wife Nellie B. Robey. Mr. and Mrs. Robey did not make this their permanent home and only lived here from March to October. The rest of the year was spent in Alexandria, Virginia. Mr. Robey worked at Potomac Yards, a railroad-switching yard, in Alexandria, Virginia. While working there, he was involved in an accident, which resulted in the loss of part of one of his legs. The loss of part of a leg did not totally stop Mr. Robey from attending to his garden, his yard, the growing of flowers and roses, and other jobs around his home. These things were accomplished with his artificial limb, use of a cane, and a wooden stool. Mrs. Robey was an accomplished seamstress during the months the couple occupied this Jermantown home. She was always busy. Mr. Robey also had a cow, a flock of chickens, and a few ducks. On the property was about 5 acres of woodland, which kept them supplied with wood for cooking and heating. When the weather was good, Mr. Robey was outside involved in the general upkeep and maintenance of his house and property. With some aid from my father, a summerhouse was erected. This was a round, cedar-pole structure, about 20 feet in diameter and 10 feet high. It had a dirt and stone floor, and openings on the side with a roof. Around most of the wall, except for a three-foot entryway, was a rough, cedar-pole bench for sitting. Out of the woods was cut a thirty-foot dead chestnut tree. This tree was dragged on the ground with a team of horses driven by my father. It was set up off the ground about 3 feet so the bark could be removed. The tree was dressed and painted white, with ropes and pulleys installed so a flag could be flown. A four-foot hole was dug and the finished pole was set in the ground. The United States flag was then flown in all its glory. Another project Mr. Robey accomplished was the erection of a scale model of his house for use as a mailbox. It was painted white and trimmed green, I think. The mailbox was set on four posts covered with latticework, and set back the appropriate distance from the traveled portion of the highway. This mailbox was a tourist attraction and many pictures and favorable comments were made.

Mr. Robey named his home "Oak Hill" and had the name outlined in flowers and flint rock. This was visible by auto traffic traveling east on Little River Turnpike. This was one of the last projects accomplished by Mr. Robey. He was a fine man. He witnessed, as a small boy, the Civil War Battle of Ox Hill, and would tell me about the battle. Mr. and Mrs. Robey had four children: Samuel, Roxie, Nellie, and Marion. The property was acquired by their daughter Nellie and her husband, David Goodnow. Only the back section, along Waples Mill Road, has been developed. The front section, facing Route 50, has not been developed, but may be included in the property to the west, which has been developed as Fairfax Ridge. The Robey house is shown on page 288 of "The Rambler," by Harry Shannon, and published by Connie P. and Mayo Stuntz.

Property 62

The property next discussed was purchased by Sampson and Ann Marie Markell Beach some years before the Civil War. It contained 60 acres, more or less. This couple was the parents of two children, Mary E. and George W. Beach. Following the Civil War, Mary E. married Stephen P. Twombly, a Union veteran from Yarmouth, Maine. George W. married Martha W. Wooster. On the death of Sampson Beach and his wife, Marie M. Beach, the two children inherited the property. All the Beach and Twombly families are interred in the Fairfax Cemetery. Mary E. Twombly sold her share of the estate to her daughter, Jobie T. Sutphin, and her husband, Ernest J. Sutphin, during 1924. All that time the size of this property was 28 acres, more or less. During 1977, the five Sutphin heirs sold this property to Georgious Company. The size of the property, at that time, contained only 21 plus acres. This was due to the loss when the Route 50/Route 66 interchange was built. Also the Sutphin children built homes on the property. The property has been developed as Fairfax Ridge. The original purchasers of this property were the Sampson Beachs. They were from Alexandria, Virginia. Before the Civil War, this couple had joined a group of people in the construction of a railroad from the port at Alexandria southwest to Fairfax Station where they were living when they acquired the original tract of land at Jermantown. The Sampson Beach family had two other children, twins, a boy and a girl. These children died in infancy and are interred at the old cemetery located at Jerusalem Baptist Church. No grave marker can be found and I have been unsuccessful in obtaining any additional information. Samuel Beach, a brother, also worked on the railroad. He and his family settled in the Lorton area. The Samuel Beach family is believed to be interred in Pohick Episcopal Church Cemetery. Of the original 60 acres of this property, almost one half stayed, for about 128 years, in one family, the Beach, Twombly and Sutphin family. Through the Civil War, Spanish American War, World War I, World War II, and the war in Korea, this property was our home before the final 21 acres were sold and developed as Fairfax Ridge.

5.13 Property 62, the Sampson Beach house. The two rooms on the east end were added after the Civil War. They were removed in 1935 and the house was rebuilt as shown in Figure 5.14.

5.14 Property 62, the Sampson Beach house when owned by E.J. and Jobie T. Sutphin. The five Sutphin children—Aubrey W., Council M., Vincent D., Musette Nevitte, and Doris Dunn—all had homes built on this property. None exist today.

CHAPTER 5   *Jermantown West*

5.15 Property 62, Fairfax Ridge. This development covers the E.J. Sutphin farm, some of the R.R. Robey property, and a small part of the R.H. Downs property. The development faces Waples Mill Road.

5.16 Property 62, Fairfax Ridge, storm flood holding pond under construction.

Nothing Remains the Same

On with my rambling, I will now tell the condition of the house and 28 acres when the Sutphin family moved here from Fairfax during November, 1924. This move was made by horse and wagon, with the assistance of a Model T Ford truck owned by my uncle, Henry Downs. The original part, or west section, of the house was a story and a half with a large fireplace on its original east end. The kitchen, one room, adjoined the north end with a separate chimney for cooking and heating. This kitchen contained a large white pine corner cupboard. On the east end enclosing the fireplace chimney, after the Civil War, were built two additional rooms. These two rooms were a full two-story, making the roofline continuous, but with a four-foot difference in the front entrance level between the new two rooms and the original old house. The new rooms had a front entrance as well, and were accessible from the old house. One could say this was the original split-level home. Four large English boxwoods stood in the front yard. These four boxwoods found their way to the Middleburg and Upperville areas of Loudoun County within five years after the Sutphin family occupied this home. Some people liked the new look and some did not. My mother did not care. She could see out and we had been well paid. All but one field was grown up in pines and other underbrush. These were cleared, the land tilled and planted. New fences were built. The barn was enlarged. New outbuildings were built, and within five to ten years the house rebuilt and electricity installed. All this was due to the efforts of my mother and father.

Again I return to the Civil War period because I heard so much about it when I was young. Also, we were well versed on this subject during courses in Virginia history and United States history in elementary school at Fairfax. I have previously mentioned the pine corner cupboard in the kitchen. My great-grandmother had a double drop-leaf mahogany table, which she inherited and was used during this period by her. This table is now owned by my sister, Musette Nevitte, and shows two large nails under the main table. This supported a small wooden leaf to hide food from both the Union and Confederate armies. The Beach family had no special time to prepare food or to eat. During the Civil War at

CHAPTER 1   The Beginning

various times two Union outposts were established, one at Milestone 16 at the top of Difficult Run Hill at the Wooster home, and one at the Jermantown Road and Little River Turnpike intersection. The Beach family was not slave owners. Son George was only 14 years old at the start of the war. During the last three years of the war, most of this area was occupied by the Union Army. Farm work and staying out of sight must have been a good occupation. Anyway it was never discussed with me. Today is different in this area. That is why I have tried so hard to tell how it was. How my people lived without taking sides because I have lived both ways. In my time the horse, buggy, and wagon were a big means of transportation. We have gone from this to the Atomic Age and placing a man on the moon. What is next is unknown. That is good, too. It is my thoughts that God did not want us to know too much.

Chapter 6

Milestone 16–Difficult Run

Property 63

This is about the remaining Samuel Beach property, which was inherited by George W. Beach. This plot of land contained 30 acres, more or less, and was sold to Clarice Craig in 1944 by the George Beach heirs. This property was farmed by Isaac Craig until the Route 50/Route 66 interchange and 66 highway constructions reduced the size of this original plot of land to about 10 acres. This property now contains three

6.1 Property 64, the famous poplar tree in Swart woods, March 1959. This tree gave shelter to many unfortunate men during the Great Depression, 1930-35.

6.2 Property 64, now 11325 Random Hills Road, built on Swart farm.

houses and several outbuildings. Ownership and development status are unknown. Milestone 16 located on Route 50, at or near the common corner between the Craig and Swart properties, is gone. These were landmarks, but unfortunately in the Route 50/Route 66 interchange construction, were lost.

Property 64

The next tract of land was owned by the Swart family. This plot of land must have contained approximately 80 to 100 acres. One field was open and farmed. This field contained a grove of chestnut trees, which were still alive and bearing in the early 1930s. This field ran along the turnpike from the top of Difficult Run Hill to almost Difficult Run and the old arch bridge. Another open field ran along the Run on both sides, almost to the Neff property line on the north. This field was included in the remainder, which was in the woods and used as a pasture for the Swart dairy herd. During the summer the Swart dairy herd was driven each morning to pasture and returned each afternoon for milking at their barn on Jermantown Road. This was a trip of about one-half mile over Route 50. The cattle were driven against auto, truck, and bus traffic. This practice was discontinued in the late 1930s, as traffic on Route 50 became too heavy to permit the continuation of this type of operation. This operation was accomplished by one person driving the cattle and one person with a red flag 100 feet in front to slow and, if necessary, stop the traffic in front of the herd. With traffic stopped, the herd could proceed on to the pasture field. During all seasons of the year this property was never idle. The neighborhood boys saw to that. We got more than our share of chestnuts and blackberries, and dammed Difficult Run in the summer for swimming. During the spring we picked wildflowers for biology classes, and did a lot of cork-and-sinker fishing. We never caught very much, but we tried. Another item that was big on our list was to explore the big, hollow poplar tree. This hollow tree had been used by men during the Depression, to spend the night. Evidence of this had been left behind such as open tins, campfire, and other trash. As previously mentioned, Difficult Run passes through this property flowing north to the Potomac River east of Great Falls. The single-arch

6.3 Property 65, the E.D. Denny home replaced the two-story frame house.
Courtesy of Mrs. Shirley Vanvleet

6.4 Property 65, the site of the E.D. Denny home today.
Courtesy of Mrs. Shirley Vanvleet

stone bridge was 15 to 20 feet over the water so Little River Turnpike could continue from Aldie to Alexandria, Virginia. It was constructed during colonial times. To the best of my knowledge, this bridge was not destroyed during the Civil War.

Property 65

This was the location of the E.D. Denny property. The original frame house and property were purchased from the Neff family during the 1930s and contained about 13 acres. The Denny family was from Waynesboro, Virginia. Before the family could move here, Mrs. Denny passed away. Misfortune continued to follow the family. Shortly after moving here, the house burned. This was a frame, two-story farmhouse, which was replaced by a brick bungalow. Mr. Denny raised chickens and truck farmed. This continued until most of the property was consumed by the Route 50/Route 66 interchange. The remaining property is in housing. After all these years, I hope I have not forgotten anyone. The Denny family members were William, Edith, Earnest, Eugene, Ellen, Annie, John, Judy, George, and David.

Property 66

In the rear of the Denny property, with an entrance and some footage along Route 50, was the location of the E.E. Neff home and dairy farm operation. This was a large tract of land and must have contained over 115 acres. Close to the end of World War II, this property was sold and developed into Fairfax Farms subdivision. On this property, marked as Property 66A in this book and just west of the stone-arch bridge over Difficult Run, were the remains of an old tollhouse for the old Little River Turnpike. Along Difficult Run, which splits the property on the north end, are the remains of the Waples Mill dam, marked here as Property 70. Due to the contour of the land on the east side of Difficult Run, large sections of this old subdivision are under redevelopment with large and expensive housing. This has helped bring about a building of trails along the run valley by the developers. The Route 50/Route 66 interchange only affected the entrance to the subdivision on the old Neff property.

6.5 Property 67, the Nathaniel Bacon home, being relocated from the north side of Route 50 to the Fairfax Farms subdivision, as a result of the construction of the Route 50/Route 66 interchange.

Property 67

This is the location of the Nathaniel Bacon home and property. Mr. Bacon and his wife were from West Virginia and purchased this property during the 1930s from the Matthews family. The Bacon family had the old frame farmhouse removed and a new, modern, brick house built. This was a nice tract of land consisting of 40 or more acres running along Little River Turnpike for over a half mile and joining the Neff property on the north. Mr. Bacon raised beautiful flowers such as gladiolas and peonies, which he sold from a roadside stand on the weekends. My father, on several occasions, cut hay off the property. Mr. and Mrs. Bacon lived on the property until both passed away. Phillip Matthews was the previous owner of the Bacon property. His daughter Sadie graduated from Oakton High School in the class of 1924. Among the first members of the Pender Methodist Church was Salome N. Matthews, who I believe was Sadie's mother. Most of this property is in the Route 50/Route 66 interchange; what property is not included is covered in housing or streets.

Chapter 7

Jermantown Area –
North Side of Warrenton Pike

My attempt to reminisce on what has occurred and who lived where will continue now along the old Warrenton Pike. We will start with its intersection with the old Little River Turnpike at Kamp Washington. Today the Warrenton Turnpike is known as Route 29 or the 29th Division Highway.

Property 101

The first piece of property was owned by the George R. Wells family. This same family may have also owned the previously discussed Property 1 in Chapter 1. This property was occupied by the Cook family before it became the Black Lantern Inn. On this property were a small frame bungalow, several outbuildings, and a small store. This store sold tobacco, soft drinks, candy, bread, and other notions. It was operated by Mr. Wells and later acquired by Mr. Chambers. In the rear of the store was a large field in which Mr. Wells would permit the playing of baseball while he was operating the store. After World War II, Mr. Shirley Lunceford acquired some of this property and built a small shopping center. This center had a restaurant and several other stores. One was the first location of the Fairfax Hardware Store. Other developers constructed the gas station and several other commercial buildings, which occupy the property today.

Property 102

The next property size is unknown. It contained a well-kept, painted, two-story frame house occupied by Winfield Runner and his brother, Ben Runner. Winfield Runner was born in Virginia in 1860. The Runner brothers were old men, and had a team of horses and a wagon. They did various jobs in the neighborhood until their deaths during the 1930s. This property is now covered by commercial development.

Property 103

This discussion brings us to the southeast corner of Jermantown Road and Route 29, or Warrenton Pike. This property was owned by Jake Colbert. His son, Clarence Colbert, and Clarence's wife lived with him. Clarence also had a team of horses, as well as a truck, and he did all types of work in the neighborhood. During the autumn and winter months, Clarence was kept busy slaughtering and dressing hogs, and doing other related farm work. Today this property is covered with commercial buildings.

Property 104

Continuing north and on the east side of Jermantown Road, the next property was owned by the Tilson family. This family moved here in the 1930s. They purchased a small piece of property and erected a small house. The family consisted of several males and two females. They all found work. I am unable to come up with their names. The property is now commercial and may include an outlet to the Dominion Power Company.

Property 105

Continuing on the east side of Jermantown Road was a small house and lot. It was owned by Charlie Scott and his wife. It joined the Swart property on the north. Some of this property may be also included in the Dominion Power Company property.

Property 106

During the 1930s, the west side of Jermantown Road, from the south property line of the Swart family property to Warrenton Pike, was one large field. From the southwest corner of Jermantown Road, west along the Warrenton Pike to Shirley Gate Road, several frame Cape Cod houses were built by a contractor, and sold by a man by the name of Riley. Before these houses were built, this field was used by Lehman Young as an airfield. Today these houses still stand. The property along Jermantown Road is now commercial. The remainder of this large field is covered in individual housing and apartments, with Waples Mill Road extending through from Route 50 to connect with Warrenton Pike at the Shirley Gate Road intersection.

7.1 Property 107, the Charles C. and Martha Rosemond home at Lee Highway and Shirley Gate Road. This house is alleged to be a precut, ready-to-assemble, Sears Roebuck house. Approximately 500 feet northwest of this house, on the old John Jerman farm, was Property 108, a former German prisoner-of-war camp during World War II.

Property 107

This is the location of the Rosemond family home and property. This family consisted of three members, Charles C., his wife Martha, and son, Charles, Jr. The Rosemond family left the area after World War II. Present property owners are unknown as is the present size, but it must consist of several acres. Some of this property is occupied by a family storage operation. The home still stands and it is said to be a Sears Roebuck house, a precut and ready to assemble house, the largest sold by them. The Rosemond family operated a poultry and egg business. The eggs were sold to large hotels in Washington, DC, and also allegedly to the White House. Today the chicken houses are gone and most of the property is occupied by the storage business. The house and several small outbuildings still stand. It is only a matter of time before this landmark will be replaced.

CHAPTER 7   *Jermantown Area – North Side of Warrenton Pike*

7.2 Property 108, this storage warehouse and the new building under construction in the background are the general location of the old State Prison Camp which was used to house the German POWs in 1945 on Lee Highway just west of the intersection of present Waples Mill Road.
Photograph by Lee Hubbard, April 2009

Property 108

This is the first location of Camp 30 of the Virginia Prison System, established in the summer of 1941 or 1942. This camp closed during World War II and reopened as a prisoner-of-war (POW) camp. The German POWs were used by Fairfax County farmers to aid them in the working of their farms, as local help was unavailable. This treatment of these POWs was approved by the Geneva Convention after the end of WWI, and applied to any future world conflicts. This POW camp was closed later in 1945 or early 1946 and reopened again as Camp 30 by the Virginia Department of Prisons for use by the Virginia Department of Highways. This temporary camp remained at this location until a new modern Camp 30 was opened on Route 608 at Legato in the 1950s. This property contains from 30 to 40 acres and is now all grown up. During the 1930s, before his death, it was part of the John Jerman farm.

Property 108A

Today this is a street named Ridge Top Road. In the past 100 years, it has been known as Mills Road, Green Lane, and Feather Bed Lane. George Beach and Stephen P. Twombly gave land to connect it to Little River Turnpike to the north, I have been told by older family members. To the best of my knowledge, until the completion of the Route 50/ Route 66 interchange and rearrangement of the entrance of Random Hill subdivision, what is now Ridge Top Road was not maintained by the Virginia Department of Highways. It was only an outlet for several houses in the same area.

Next in our discussion is a long rectangular piece of property containing 10 or more acres, on which stood a house. This property was, at one time, owned by Dr. Kate Waller Barrett. The next owner with whom I am familiar was an English lady by the name of Eliott, who ran a summer boarding school for young girls. The property would be closed in fall, winter, and spring. The next owners were Mr. and Mrs. L.H. Green. The Greens had electricity, telephones, and a bathroom installed, as well as other improvements. Mr. L.H. Green worked for the government. Mr. and Mrs. Green were divorced, and the next owner was a Miss Mary O. Ambler, a schoolteacher in the Fairfax County Public School system. I lose knowledge of further property ownership. Today the property is covered with large commercial buildings. During the Civil War, this property was used as a burying ground from the hospital on the Stephen P. Twombly property, as previously discussed. It is my thought that after Dr. Kate Waller Barrett sold this property, she acquired property in what is now the City of Fairfax, as well as the Ivakota farm near Clifton, Virginia.

Property 108B

The George Beach family owned property on the west side of Ridge Top Road, from Route 50 on the north to the John Jerman farm on the south. This property contained 90 acres, plus or minus, and it covered a distance of about one-half mile. The Beach property is covered in my

CHAPTER 7   *Jermantown Area – North Side of Warrenton Pike*

discussion of the Little River Turnpike review. The Beach heirs sold one piece of property to a Mr. Ramsey with a frontage on Ridge Top Road. It contained 5 acres more or less. The remaining property was sold to the developers of Random Hill subdivision and the highway department for the Route 50/Route 66 interchange.

Property 108C

Mr. and Mrs. Louie Robertson owned a small piece of land, probably containing from 1 to 4 acres between the Beach and John Jerman tracts of land. The Robertson family rented this property. The house was a small frame one-and-a-half story building containing four or more rooms. There were also several outbuildings and a well house on this property. During the 1920s and 1930s, the Elmer Jerman, the Keen, and the Tom Blevins families lived here. Other families also, but I cannot recall their names now. Mr. and Mrs. Robertson lived here, as well as their son, Richard, and his wife. This property is now covered by housing.

Property 108D

Another small house and lot were occupied by the Ellis family. This property was off the old John Jerman property and was only occupied for a period of five to ten years. Today it is covered by modern housing.

Property 108E

This is the site of the John Jerman farm and house as I knew it during the 1920s through the 1950s. This was not a working farm. Mr. Jerman ran a real estate agency, and he passed away during the early 1930s. During the early 1930s, this farm was cleared, but by the 1950s it was completely grown up in second growth timber and underbrush. The house had been occupied by renters over the past years. This house was built prior to the Civil War. The house was located on the west side of Ridge Top Road and a large red barn was on the east side. These are the only two buildings I can remember. The only renters of the house I can remember are Berkeley and Maude R. Kidwell and family. The total size of this piece of property must have been more than 100 acres. It ran along Route 29 for about a half a mile to Difficult Run on the west, and north along Difficult Run to the Beach line, along the Beach line east to the Rosemond line, and south along the Rosemond line until the point of beginning. All the property has housing today except the wooded section east of Ridge Top Road, on which the old German POW Camp was located. It is my understanding that this is now under construction for development, and efforts are being made to mark the prison location.

This will end my review of the north side of Route 29 property owners of the past in the Jermantown area. We will return to the Kamp Washington area and start on the south side of the old Warrenton Pike, or Route 29, for further review of property owners.

Chapter 8

Jermantown Area –
South Side of Warrenton Pike

Property 129

During the late 1920s, at the intersection of Little River Turnpike and the Warrenton Pike at Kamp Washington, on the south side, was located a large, frame, two-story house. This house was occupied by Will and Lillie Smith and other members of their family. Ownership and size of this property are unknown. During the late 1930s, this property was acquired by Albert Sherwood. The house was removed and the property cleared. The house was replaced with a large two-story brick home. This property today is occupied by several commercial enterprises. The large brick house has been relocated in a housing development.

Property 130

The next property I review was owned by Douglas McFarland and his wife, who taught school in the Fairfax County system. Mr. McFarland was an electrical contractor and he was one of the first to be licensed by Fairfax County. This lot and house were small. The house was of frame construction. Also visible from this location, on a clear day, was the top of the Washington Monument, but no longer. Today this property is occupied by commercial building.

Property 131

This was the location of a black family on the east corner of Warrenton Pike and Rust Road. This was not a large lot. The house was of frame construction. The house and lot were well kept, with a good-size garden spot and yard. I have been unsuccessful in coming up with the family's name. The property today is occupied by a gas station.

Property 132

The next property on the east side of Rust Road was owned by Washington and Charity Payne. This was not a big lot. It contained a small frame house and garden spot. This couple was old and had to accept what work they could. The couple was well respected by their neighbors, who provided some aid. Today the property is occupied by commercial buildings and several houses. All are located in the City of Fairfax.

CHAPTER 8 *Jermantown Area – South Side of Warrenton Pike*

Property 133
We return to the Warrenton Pike and Rust Road area and start my review of the west side of this location. During the 1920s and 1930s, this property was unoccupied. The house was in a run-down condition and vacant. Mr. Miller Kielsgard acquired this property after World War II. He had the house removed and had a small temporary-type building erected for living quarters, which he occupied until his death due to an automobile accident. This property is now part of a shopping area.

Property 134
The next property on the west side of Rust Road was owned by Frank Blevins and his wife. Mr. Blevins owned a dump truck and worked for the Virginia Department of Highways. Today this property is under development and several large houses are under construction, or have been completed and are ready for sale.

Property 135
The next property was owned by Durley and Leish Sutphin and members of their family. Today this property is under development. Large houses are under construction and several have been completed and are ready for sale.

Property 136
The next property on the west side of Rust Road, as I knew it in the 1930s, was an abandoned stone quarry. The stone removed proved to be of low quality. It was too soft for use on the reconstruction of the Warrenton Pike in the 1920s. This property is under development to be occupied by a large housing unit.

Property 137
During the 1920s, a large farm here was owned and occupied by the Harry Mills family. It was accessible at the end of Rust Road. This was a good-size farm of perhaps 50 or more acres. After Mr. Mills' death, this property was acquired by Mr. John Rust, and today is occupied

Nothing Remains the Same

by modern housing and streets in the City of Fairfax. The remains of a private, stone-walled cemetery may be viewed today. This cemetery contained the remains of a Confederate veteran, Sgt. James Haley of the 1st Virginia Infantry and other members of the Haley family. This property was owned before and after the Civil War by the Haley family. The house that occupied this property was a large two-story frame structure with a large, impressive brick chimney. I cannot recall the chimney's location, whether on the end or the middle of the house. I only visited this property several times while the house was standing and the property had not been developed. During the late 1930s, my uncle John and aunt Kate Sutphin farmed this tract of land before moving to the Willow Springs and the Catlett, Virginia, areas. This property is covered in housing and in the corporate limits of the City of Fairfax. Some remains of the old family cemetery located on 4422 San Carlos Drive, Fairfax, Virginia, may be viewed today.

Property 138

This next piece of property I know very little about. The only occupants were the Mulhollands. The size of the property could not have been large because the frontage on the Warrenton Pike could not have been more than 600 feet. Two sons of this family were veterans of the Civil War. Their names were John and Pete. The property is now included in a shopping center.

Property 139

The next property was owned by Gladys Winfield. Mrs. Winfield was a business lady who operated a real estate and property rental business from her home in the Legato and Fairfax area. There were several houses on this property, which were rented. Mrs. Winfield occupied a large two-story frame home. After her death during World War II, Mr. A.B. Stanley acquired this property. He was also in the real estate business. Today the property is covered by shopping centers, mobile homes, and other commercial buildings.

CHAPTER 8   *Jermantown Area – South Side of Warrenton Pike*

Property 140

The Mickelson family occupied the east corner of Shirley Gate Road and Warrenton Pike. The house occupying this corner was of frame, two-story construction, and set close to the traveled highway. I have been told that the Mickelson family came to Virginia from the Midwest before 1910. Mr. Mickelson was in the poultry and egg business. The Mickelson family had two children, a son and a daughter. The daughter, Ethel M. Dennis, worked for Fairfax County for a number of years until her retirement. She also was one of 10 students who graduated from the old Oakton High School in the class of 1926. After Mr. Mickelson's death, this property, containing the house and outbuildings, was split and sold. Herb Welsh became the owner of the original house and some acres. He opened a store in the house and built tourist cabins backing up to Shirley Gate Road. None of this remains today, as a storage business occupies some of this property. The remaining property was acquired by daughter Ethel M. Dennis, who had a house built and lived there until selling and moving to the City of Fairfax, where she lived until her death. Today the property is occupied by a bank and also may contain some housing on the rear with access to and from streets off Shirley Gate Road.

Property 140A

This was a small lot and house on the east side of Shirley Gate Road. The owner was Corbin O'Bannon and his wife, whose name I think was Lizzy. This property was acquired by the O'Bannons during the late thirties, and it was their second home. This property today is covered with modern housing.

Property 140B

This was a small lot and house owned by Ester Robey Carpender and her husband Charles. This property was located on the east side of Shirley Gate Road, approximately one-quarter of a mile from the Warrenton Pike. Mrs. Carpender was a cousin on my father's side of our family. This property was sold and the family relocated to Warrenton, Virginia.

8.1 Property 140C, the Ed Moore home on Shirley Gate Road.
Courtesy of Agnes Moore

The property is now covered with large modern housing. No further review of the east side of Shirley Gate Road will be made, as I am not familiar with the ownership.

Property 140C

We will review the west side of Shirley Gate Road north to the Warrenton Pike. The first piece of property was seven-and-one-half acres owned by Edward B. and Mattie Sutphin Moore. This couple was my uncle and aunt from my father's side of our family. This property contained a small, log, one-story house when acquired from Mr. Moore's mother during the 1930s. The house was enlarged and improvements made on the wooded lot, as my uncle was a hard-working man doing construction work as a painter. He was also a veteran of World War I and he was proud of his service to his country. His son, George R. Moore, served in World War II. Both are interred in Fairfax's cemetery. After the death of my Aunt Mattie, the property was sold. Four acres were sold for housing and the remaining to a Korean church located at 1400 Shirley Gate Court. Members of the Moore family are George R. Moore,

CHAPTER 8   *Jermantown Area – South Side of Warrenton Pike*

Mary Agnes Fendley, Barbara Rowland, Phillip H. Moore, and Mayonie Bradford. Today an old section of the original Shirley Gate Road has been renamed Mattie Moore Court. This was accomplished after zoning and street renaming by Fairfax County and the family.

8.2   Property 141, the old Silver Moon Restaurant at the corner of Lee Highway and Shirley Gate Road, after it had been veneered in brick. The building was removed in 2005 after being unoccupied for a number of years. In 1940 a cold Budweiser cost 35 cents and a Coke cost 5 cents.

Property 140D

During the 1930s, all property north of Ed and Mattie Moore's property on the west side of Shirley Gate Road to the Warrenton Pike was owned by Ed Moore's mother, Alice Morris Moore. It must have contained more than 10 to 15 acres and was sold at an auction. This property today is covered with about 50 houses, more or less. These houses are located on Peep Toad Court, Nancy Ann Way, Delsignore, and Shirley Gate Court.

Property 141

This is the location of the old Silver Moon Restaurant on about one acre of land, more or less. This building was of frame construction with parking in the front. It was built during the late 1930s and was in operation until the early 1960s. The building was removed in 2005 after being vacant and in a deteriorating condition. Today the lot is cleared and unoccupied.

8.3 Property 142, currently a nursery and plant business on Lee Highway near Shirley Gate Road, this building was originally constructed as a Texaco gas station, 1938-39. The Fairfax Volunteer Fire Department held numerous turkey shoots in the rear of the building on Saturday afternoons 1938-40.

8.4 Property 143, the former home of Corbin and Lizzy O'Bannon. Today this is part of the plant business on Lee Highway near Shirley Gate Road.

CHAPTER 8   *Jermantown Area – South Side of Warrenton Pike*

Property 142
This is the location of a stone building built and used as a gas station during the late 1930s and 1940s. This building and grounds are occupied as a nursery and plant business.

Property 143
The next property was once owned by Harriet Lamb Carter, who had a sister, Annie Mills, and a son, George Carter. This property was acquired by the son George, who sold some of the land to Corbin O'Bannon and his wife Lizzy. I hope I have Mrs. O'Bannon's name correct. Mr. O'Bannon worked as a carpenter and roofer. The O'Bannons had at least one son, Cecil. Other family members, if any, are unknown. During the late 1930s, this property was sold to parties I cannot recall, and the O'Bannons acquired the property on the east side of Shirley Gate Road, previously discussed at Property 140A. Today the house still stands, and the property is occupied as a nursery operation. It is my understanding that following the Civil War, Harriet Lamb Carter and her sister, Annie Mills, contributed to the acquisition of what is now known as the Jermantown Cemetery.

Property 144
The next piece of property was a small lot with a frame house owned by Ira Roberson and his wife, Ann Cronk. The Robersons were married in 1895 and had two daughters, Elsie and Edith, and one son, Oswald. I only knew Mr. Roberson, as his wife had passed away before my time. During the time of this discussion, this house and property were occupied by Ira, his brother George, his sister Maggie Richardson, and her husband, William. Mr. Richardson was older than the others by some five to ten years. Today the house no longer stands. The property is grown up and I am not familiar with who owns the property.

Property 145
On the southeast corner of the Warrenton Pike and what is now Forrest Hill Drive stood a story-and-a-half dwelling of frame construction.

When my family moved to the Jermantown area, this house and property were owned by Greenberry Cronk and his wife, Sara J. Thompson. The Cronks were the owners of several acres of land in this general area, and this was said to be about 10 acres. During the Civil War, Mr. Cronk's father was the operator of a tollgate on the Warrenton Pike. Also, he is alleged to have raised the gate so Colonel John S. Mosby and his famous prisoner, General Stoughton, could pass through. No toll was charged. I checked this with Ann Dawson Nachman, Mr. Cronk's great-granddaughter, and she informed me she had been told this by members of her family, and as far as she could tell me, this was the truth. After Mr. Cronk's death in 1932, the property was acquired by his granddaughter, Elsie R. Dawson, and her husband, Tom Dawson. Mr. Dawson was a veteran of World War I and worked at the Washington Navy Yard as a crane operator. The Dawson family members were Jane, Margaret Brown, Thomas, Edwin, Ann V. Nachman, and Sara Eileen Brown. South of the Dawson home on Forrest Hill Drive, the Dawsons sold one acre of property to Mr. and Mrs. B. Aylor. The Aylors had a small house built and lived at this location for a period of time. The house no longer exists and the property is grown up. It will only be a short period of time before that property will be cleared and built upon.

Property 146

The next property was a long, rectangular piece of property running about 1,000 feet in depth and about a half-mile long, from Forrest Hill Drive on the east to Difficult Run on the west, and from Warrenton Pike on the north to the old railroad bed on the south, or to the Sherwood line. It probably contained more than 15 acres. Today a large assisted living building called "The Gardens" occupies this property, and another large building is under construction. In the past, I have been told this property was owned by Milton Jerman, who ran a slaughterhouse and butchering business along Difficult Run where the run passes through the old railroad bed. During the 1930s, the remains of a building were at this general location, but are no longer visible today. Mr. Jerman is believed to have been a brother to Rose J. Haines from the Jermantown area, and was a Confederate soldier. Mr. Jerman was also active in community affairs.

CHAPTER 8   *Jermantown Area – South Side of Warrenton Pike*

8.5   Property 146A, the George Sherwood family home.
Courtesy of Lee Hubbard

8.6   Property 146A, the George Sherwood family home.
Courtesy of Lee Hubbard

Nothing Remains the Same   **87**

Property 146A

The original owners of the Sherwood property were Louis F. and Sarah E. Kidwell Sherwood. Their children were:

Margaret E. Sherwood	1871
Laura E. Sherwood	1875
Elizabeth Sherwood	1876
George F. Sherwood	1877
Albert R. Sherwood	1879
Luther R. Sherwood	1885
Joseph R. Sherwood	?

My mother was born during the same period and was a good friend and schoolmate at Jermantown grade school, as it was so called. I write about this because from what I have been told, schoolmate friendships were life lasting, which I know to be true. After the deaths of the Louis Sherwoods, the original house and farm became the property of George and Minnie Waple Sherwood. This couple worked this property as a general farm, raising cattle as well as growing crops and garden products for market. Other members of this family are discussed in various reviews made by me, and have had an important input on community life in Jermantown, Pender, and Fairfax. The size of this farm was said to be from 40 to 60 acres. The main outlet to the property was along what is now Forest Hill Drive. Another outlet was through the Mills or Swart properties on the west. The north boundary was along the unfinished pre-Civil War railroad bed. This house was a large, two-story, log, weatherboard home. In the front yard was a large full-flowing spring, the headwaters of Difficult Run, which empties into the Potomac River east of Great Falls. The old house, as well as the spring, has been destroyed by the final development of this property. After World War II, Fred and Bramwell Kielsgard acquired the Sherwood property and developed it into Kielsgarden subdivision, selling lots for the construction of houses, setting aside the original house and a few acres of land for private ownership. The property included a man-made lake, using the old railroad embankment for a dam. Today the lake remains, but the old

CHAPTER 8   *Jermantown Area – South Side of Warrenton Pike*

house is gone and some 20 to 25 large, expensive houses have been built on the original property that was set aside for the old house and private lake. During my time the George and Minnie Sherwood family members were as follows:

>   Franklin Sherwood
>   Vernon Sherwood
>   Gladys Sherwood Downs
>   Alvin Sherwood
>   Lewis Sherwood
>   Isabell Sherwood Campbell
>   Howard Sherwood
>   Walter Sherwood

This ends my review of the Jermantown area. This family, as all the other families I have discussed, had a part and played that part to the best of their ability in the so-called development of this area. The biggest change came after two wars, the Civil War and World War II, in my opinion. One can only guess what it was before the Civil War. I leave it to others to tell what it will be like after this.

Chapter 9

The Church and School at Pender

9.1 Property 21, the Millan/Bryce/Thompson farm, now the location of Fair Oaks Mall.

9.2 Property 21, the Millan/Bryce/Thompson farm, now the location of Fair Oaks Mall.

CHAPTER 9 *The Church and School at Pender*

9.3   Property 21, the Millan/Bryce/Thompson farm as seen from the yard of Pender Methodist Church, Property 23, in 1960.

9.4   Property 21, the Millan/Bryce/Thompson farm as a golf course, now the location of Fair Oaks Mall.

Property 21

Our review will start on the left side of the Little River Turnpike, east of one of the highest points of Fairfax County. We begin at what was known as the Thomas Millan farm, then the Bryce family farm, and, during my time, as the Albert and Florence Thompson dairy farm. The Bryce family moved to this location from New York prior to the Civil War. The house was a large two-story, frame, weatherboard house with front porches. It may have stood before the Civil War. The Thompson family sold most of the farm after World War II, and the farm was converted to a golf course before its final conversion to Fair Oaks Shopping Center and the Route 50/Route 66 interchange. After this conversion, the Thompson family built three new homes on the rear of the farm, along Random Hills Road, on the remaining section of their farm.

Property 21A

This is the location of the Ira Hutchinson home and a small plot of land. Mr. Hutchinson married Elizabeth C. Fletcher. Their children were: Randolph; Lillian, who married Martin Everhart from Loudoun County; and Aubrey W., 1918-1973, whose marriage status is unknown. Aubrey was among one of the first to be drafted from Fairfax County during World War II and ended same with a corporal rank. His brother, Randolph, also served during World War II and was killed in action in Europe. His remains were returned and interred in the Fairfax Cemetery. Today this property is part of the Fair Oaks Shopping Center.

Property 22

The old Legato Road used to connect with the Little River Turnpike east of the old Pender Methodist Church. The location of the old church is now occupied by a large modern building known as the Pender Veterinary Clinic. The north end of Legato Road connects to this building, other building parking lots, and service areas. Another section of Legato Road connects to West Ox Road in this same general area. The south end of what remains of the old Legato Road now connects to Fair

CHAPTER 9   *The Church and School at Pender*

9.5   Property 23, Pender Methodist Church 50th anniversary pamphlet.

9.6   Property 23, the steeple from the old Pender Methodist Church, in a park area near the old location of the church.

Nothing Remains the Same   **95**

9.7   Property 23, the steeple from the old Pender Methodist Church. Located in small park.

Lakes Parkway. Several families lived on this section of Legato Road. The ones I am familiar with are the Frank Stewart, the L.H. Green, the Mozingo, and the Wallace and Madeline Cross families. The only remaining original building is the Center Point Church at Fair Oaks.

Property 23

This is the location of the Old Pender Methodist Church. This was a frame building, and the history of it is discussed in a pamphlet written by Alvin Birch and Melvin Lee Steadman, Jr., for the church's *Fifty Golden Years*. The printing was by the Virginia Press of Fairfax, Virginia. The old church has been removed from the location. The property was included in the Route 50, West Ox Road, Route 608 interchange and overpass and commercial development in the area.

CHAPTER 9   *The Church and School at Pender*

9.8   Property 24, Ernest Gheen general store, Pender, Virginia.
Courtesy of Ray Birch

Property 23A
This is the Ox Road overpass of Route 50 and its interchange.

Property 24
This is the location of the Ernest Gheen store and house. This was a large building, with the store on the east end of the house. Mr. Gheen ran the store for a number of years. Mr. and Mrs. Gheen were the parents of three children: Jack; Irene; and Maurice, who married Louise Bowman.

Property 25
This is the location of the Tommie Kidwell blacksmith shop. Mr. Kidwell was a very talented blacksmith and it was always a treat for me to visit his shop. He did not have a large spreading chestnut tree, but had a very large white oak tree at his shop. Conversations between Mr. Kidwell and my father contained all the local gossip, which I was not allowed to repeat. Mr. Kidwell was very

talented when it came to playing the violin, and many, including myself, remembered his lively tunes at dances in homes in the neighborhood. The Kidwell family consisted of Leish, who married Durley Sutphin; Elsie, who married E. Staats; Archie, who married Christine Bowman; Berkley, who married Maude Roberson; and Wesley, who married Ethel Makley.

Property 25A

The Kidwell home was located in the woods directly in back of the shop. I never had the opportunity to visit this home, and do not have any idea what it looked like. Tommie Kidwell was married to Rose E. Lightfoot.

Property 26

This is the location of the Thompson farm tenant house. Gilbert, one of the Thompson family sons, remodeled this house after World War II. He made it his home for only a few years, after which he built a larger house on the rear of what remained of the old family farm.

9.9 Property 26A, the Max Sherwood Store at Pender, 1937. Buildings no longer exist.
Courtesy of Mrs. Shirley Vanvleet

CHAPTER 9   *The Church and School at Pender*

9.10 Property 26A, Max Sherwood property. Buildings no longer exist. *Courtesy of Mrs. Shirley Vanvleet*

Property 26A

The next property was purchased by Maxwell Sherwood after his marriage to Edith Denny during the 1930s. The Sherwoods erected a small brick house with an adjoining brick store and fruit stand. The size of this property is unknown, and after several years the Sherwoods sold it and moved to the Falls Church area.

Properties 27, 28, and 28A

The next three houses were owned by members of the Louis M. and Carrie Thompson families. Family members were Louis, Elsie, Elbert, Ethel, and Willie. None of these homes remain today. The Thompson family operated a sawmill business. The steam unit they used was portable, with a planer. They also used a one-and-a-half-ton truck to deliver their saleable lumber to customers, which was ahead of the 1930s times.

Nothing Remains the Same

9.11 An example illustrating the general sawmill business as practiced by Mr. Louis Thompson on Properties 27, 28, and 28A, and Mr. Fielding Byrne on Property 29. This particular photo is not from the Pender area.

9.12 An example illustrating the general sawmill business as practiced by Mr. Louis Thompson on Properties 27, 28, and 28A, and Mr. Fielding Byrne on Property 29. This particular photo is not from the Pender area.

CHAPTER 9   *The Church and School at Pender*

9.13 An example illustrating the general sawmill business as practiced by Mr. Louis Thompson on Properties 27, 28, and 28A, and Mr. Fielding Byrne on Property 29. This particular photo is not from the Pender area.

9.14 An example illustrating the general sawmill business as practiced by Mr. Louis Thompson on Properties 27, 28, and 28A, and Mr. Fielding Byrne on Property 29. This particular photo is not from the Pender area.

Nothing Remains the Same   **101**

9.15 An example illustrating the general sawmill business as practiced by Mr. Louis Thompson on Properties 27, 28, and 28A, and Mr. Fielding Byrne on Property 29. This particular photo is not from the Pender area.

Property 29

The next property was owned by Mr. Fielding Littleton Byrne, 1852-1932, and his wife, Minnie Lambert, 1861-1928. The size of this property is unknown, but it must have consisted of several acres. Mr. Byrne ran a steam-powered sawmill with a planer. The water for the steam engine came from a small stream on the property. Mr. Byrne had a small earth-and-slab dam constructed to create a small pond about 3 feet deep and 10 to 15 feet long to provide the necessary water for the steam engine. If at all possible, I would try to be available for a trip to this fantastic place with my father and his team of horses. After Mr. Byrne's death, the sawmill operation was discontinued and a restaurant was built. This operated for a short period of time and the building was remodeled as a dwelling. This dwelling was occupied during World War II by the McCarthy family. This family lost two sons during World War II. Any remarks of condolence by me will never replace the loss by the family of William M. McCarthy and his brother, Joe McCarthy.

CHAPTER 9 *The Church and School at Pender*

Property 30

This was the location of the Fielding L. and Minnie L. Byrne home.

9.16 Property 31, the old Pender School, closed circa 1924.
Photographer unknown; Courtesy the V.D. Sutphin collection

Property 31

This was the location of the old Pender School. The size of this property is unknown. Around 1924 this school was closed and the children from the Pender area were transported by bus to the new Fairfax Elementary and one-year high school. Fairfax County provided transportation for the closed Pender, Jermantown, Hatmark, and Merrifield schools. Fairfax County purchased a new Model T school bus that was driven by Roy Croson of Pender, and later by Vernon Kidwell. Transportation before this time was provided by Fairfax County, but the bus was owned by Mr. Miller S. Kielsgard, driver unknown, but is believed to have been Mark Weller. The property on which this school was built may have been purchased from the Byrne family. After the school was closed, the building was turned into a dwelling. When Route 50 was made into four lanes, it was removed.

Property 32

Mr. Louis Thompson, Jr., built a good-size, modern home at the intersection of Dorforth Drive, Little River Turnpike, and Route 50 during the late 1930s. This couple had their own family by then. This home no longer exists and the property is covered with modern housing.

Property 33

All male members of the Thompson family were involved in the operation of the sawmill business during the 1920s, 1930s, and early 1940s. As Mr. Louis Thompson aged, Louis Thompson, Jr., took over more of the general operation of the business. During the 1930s, he married a widow by the name of Nork who had a daughter, Louise, and a son, Auther. Mr. and Mrs. Louis Thompson and her two children moved into a large, frame home at the end of what was to become Dorforth Drive. The road is now abandoned by Fairfax County. Dorforth Drive was also an outlet for the old tour bus company named Franklin Bus Company. This company was located in the rear of the old home, which no longer exists. The whole area is now covered with modern housing.

Property 33A

The next property was owned by my great-uncle, Ed Moore, and his wife. The size of the property is unknown. The house was a two-story, frame, unpainted, weatherboard structure. The Moore family consisted of Ed, James, Nora, John, Mike, and Kate. Mr. Ed Moore had a team of horses and did odd jobs in the neighborhood. What other means of support the family may have had is unknown. My great-grandfather on my father's side was James W. Moore. He was a Confederate veteran of the 15th Virginia Cavalry. He was born in 1829 and passed away in 1915. He and his wife are interred at Manassas Cemetery. His wife, Julie R., 1834-1909, preceded him in death. I have a copy of his request for pension at the age of 85 years. He owned nothing and lived with his son near Pender. This pension application is dated February 4, 1914. The length of time spent by my great-grandfather with my uncle and aunt is unknown. Several distant cousins of the Moore and Spaulding family lived with my uncle, and attended elementary school at Fairfax in the same period I did.

Property 34

The location of the Sylvester Fox house and property is our next discussion. My memory does not permit me to recall anything about this house and the amount of property. I do recall a small refreshment stand erected out of rough lumber, where Mr. Fox sold ice-cold soft drinks to tourists and anyone who would purchase some from him along Route 50. Mr. Fox was active in the Pender Methodist Church in his younger years when the church was first organized. The Fox family consisted of a son, Otis, who did general hauling and was in the ice business during the late 1920s; Nora, a daughter, with whom I am unfamiliar; and another daughter, Mamie, who I have been told taught at Navy School and may have also taught school at Pender. Mamie married Winter Sutphin, a distant cousin of my family. The Sutphins were the parents of one son, Everett, who served in the army during World War II in the 29th Division and drove a truck. His residence was in the Fredericksburg area at the time I was writing these memories.

Property 35

Raymond and Eva S. Webster were the next property owners. Their son, Charles, and daughter, Sarah, occupied the next house in what I term the Pender area. This house was of frame construction, well kept up, and the property was clear and well cared for. What Mr. Webster did for a living, I do not recall, other than occasionally working for Harry Craig and attending to his property. Son Charles Webster, after World War II, built a Cape Cod frame house on the west part of his parents' property. He and his wife lived there until after his retirement and the property was sold. They moved from the area.

Property 35A

Alvin and Mary James Birch were the occupants of this property. The family consisted of Melvin, Ray, Phyllis Smith, and Ralph. The family home sat approximately 1,000 feet off the Little River Turnpike and Route 50, and contained 50.5 acres. This would have located the majority of the property just west of the Fairfax County Parkway. Mr. Birch made his living as a carpenter, working with Mr. Allder, George Byrne, Mr. G. Sheets, and for both Mr. Albert and Luther Sherwood. Mr. Alvin Birch was a very active member of the Pender Methodist Church. During the church's Fifty Golden Years celebration, he took an active part in the research and writing of its history, as well as other assignments during the celebration in 1959. Ray Birch, his son, is a good friend of mine and helped me with this article on the Birch family. He also has agreed to write the following essay titled "A Beech Tree." During World War II, Melvin and Ray were in the service. Melvin was with the 27th Infantry of the 25th Division and was at Schofield Barracks in Hawaii on December 7, 1941. He had many battle stars and was commissioned in the field by General Douglas MacArthur. He retired as a major. Ray served with the Second Marine Division and was in Pearl Harbor when the war ended. He served in the occupation of Japan and saw both Nagasaki and Hiroshima with the Marines. This information was furnished by Ray Birch. Ray, besides reviewing this article and adding to the same, has given me permission to reprint his essay:

A BEECH TREE
By Ray M. Birch

It was a magnificent tree. It reached over 100 feet into the air and towered over all the trees around. It was straight and well-shaped, with very smooth bark. Its diameter was at least 4½ feet. There was a majesty about it. Joyce Kilmer could have been thinking about one like this when he penned his poem "Trees," and he was right when he wrote, "Only God can make a tree." It grew along Big Rocky Run within the park area that is now part of the Greenbriar subdivision. There were many smaller beech trees around it, which I presume were its offspring. I've been told that beech trees can live to be 200 years old in this area, which would account for a lot of proliferation. It was the tallest and largest living tree in the woods where I roamed as a child. When my father showed this tree to me early in my life, he joked that it was useless to try to shoot a squirrel out of the top, because the shotgun didn't have power to reach that high.

The size alone made this an exceptional tree, but in addition to its size, the thing that was unique was that it had a carving, "H.R.M., Co. B. 25M," and the date of 1863. My father had first seen this when he was a young boy and had a curiosity about it. Many of our Sunday afternoon walks, often with visitors, took us by the tree. My father would tell about the initials and wish he knew the circumstances and who had done the carving. He read all that he could find about the Civil War in hopes of finding clues to the initials. As he became older, it became an obsession with him. He wanted to know who this person was. Sometime in the late 1960s he met Ralph Van Buskirk at the Pender Methodist Church, who offered to look in the archives to see what he could find. The story began to unfold.

The 25th Maine Infantry was in this area in 1863, and came from the Portland area. They enlisted for a nine-month tour and were formed on September 29, 1862. They reached the Washington area on October 18, 1862. They were stationed at Camp Tom Casey, Virginia. They were deployed five miles west of Fairfax Courthouse in March 1863, reaching Camp Chantilly on March 25, 1863, for picket duty along Little River Turnpike. They were mustered out on July 10, 1863. Further research provided the roster of Company B, and Lt. Hollis R. Mountfort was discovered. The story could have ended here, but it still gnawed at my father. He wanted to know more.

Over the years, many persons came to see my father for interviews about local history. Bernard W. Poirier, Director of Iroquois Research Institute of Fairfax, was one of them. In 1978 my father took him to see the tree and the initials and told him the story. My father wondered if any of Lt. Mountfort's relatives were still living. Mr. Poirier had an idea, and an article was placed in the Portland newspaper for anyone related to Lt. Mountfort to get in touch with Alvin Birch. As Paul Harvey says in his news broadcast, "Here's the rest of the story."

In July 1978, Mrs. Alice L. Shaw from Gray, Maine, wrote that she was the granddaughter of Lt. Hollis Randall Mountfort, known as Rand at home, and gave this information. He was born in 1836. He was blonde and stood slightly over 6 feet. After his tour of service with the 25th Maine Infantry, he returned and married Roxanna A. Leighton. Later he went to sea as a ship's carpenter. He was at sea when Mrs. Shaw's mother was born in 1865. He sired three sons and two daughters. Mrs. Shaw's mother was his oldest child. Mrs. Shaw describes him as being rather blunt in his conversation, and he said what he thought. His favorite expression when he was disgusted at anything was "Good GAWD." He often would say, "the gol darned thing won't go." He operated a water-powered sawmill that was in the family for three generations. The mill is no longer operational, but is still standing, now in a recreation area in West Cumberland, Maine. Lt. Mountfort died in 1925.

My father and Mrs. Shaw corresponded over several years, exchanging pictures, leaves from the tree, and other general information. Mrs. Shaw's arthritis prevented her from coming to Virginia to view the tree, although she expressed a desire to do so. She also had an intriguing story involving Gray, Maine, from the Civil War. In 1862 the family of Lt. Charles H. Colley of Co. B, 10th

CHAPTER 9   *The Church and School at Pender*

Maine Volunteers, was notified that their son had been killed in the battle of Cedar Mountain, Virginia, and the remains would be forwarded to Gray at the family's expense. The family made the necessary arrangements for bringing the body home for a proper burial. When the coffin was opened for viewing, it was found it did not contain the remains of Lt. Colley, but those of an unknown and unidentifiable Confederate soldier. After several futile attempts to determine the identity of the unknown soldier, a group of Gray's local ladies arranged to have the body buried among the members of the 10th Maine Volunteers. A few weeks later, the body of Lt. Colley arrived in Gray and was buried in the Colley family lot. Upon hearing of the confusion of the deceased soldiers, another group of ladies from the South provided funds for the white marble stone that was engraved and erected over the unknown soldier's grave. Research concluded that both Lt. Colley and the unknown soldier were wounded at the Battle for Cedar Mountain, and died at the Army hospital in Alexandria, Virginia. Each year the Confederate soldier's grave receives the same careful attention as the graves of all the other fallen heroes buried in the Gray Village Cemetery. Mrs. Shaw sees this grave often, as it is near her father's cemetery plot. It seems it really is a "small world." I wrote to Mrs. Shaw in August, 1984 and informed her of my father's death. She wrote back and expressed her sorrow and sympathy. That was the last of the correspondence.

A storm in the late 1970s broke out the top part of the beech tree. From that point on, it began to deteriorate badly. The Fairfax County Park Authority took borings and tried to determine if anything could be done to save the tree. In conjunction with the U.S. Forestry Service, they concluded the task was hopeless and chose instead to cut out a section of the tree that included the initials and treat it with ethylene glycol to preserve it. This was done. The Park Authority still has the initials in storage and hopes to put them on display at some point in time. Now all we need to do is wait another 200 years and see if one of those offspring lives to equal its parent. I doubt it will.

We now return to the main crossing of West Ox Road, the Little River Turnpike, and Route 50 to review the north side of Route 50 and both sections of West Ox Road as I remember them, and have attempted to discuss to the best of my ability.

Chapter 10

Pender

Property 68

This tract of land is located on the north side of Route 50, or Little River Turnpike, and during the 1920s and 1930s, it must have contained more than 100 acres. During this period, the property was owned by the Smith brothers, who were in the timber business, which consisted of pulpwood, railroad tiles, poles for electric and telephone lines, and timber for lumber. The eastern section was the location of the Sam Robey house, which after the Civil War was moved by wagon to the Jermantown area. Also, in the general area across from the Ira Hutchinson home, was Milestone 17 on Little River Turnpike. This landmark is long gone. After World War II, this property was developed as Penderbrook subdivision. The development of the Fair Oaks shopping area and the Route 50/Route 66 interchange had some input on the subdivision development, but not too bad, as it contains a well-planned golf course and very diversified housing.

10.1 Property 46, the Milton Tinder house at Route 50 and West Ox Road, 1960.

Property 46

This was the location of the Milton and Bertie Tinder house and property. This house and property were located on the northeast corner of West Ox Road and Little River Turnpike in a grove of large oak trees. The house was of frame construction with a steep-pitched, A-frame roof, which covered several upstairs rooms. Mr. Tinder worked at various jobs and was considered a top hand or the best you could get to do the job. The known family members are William, Myrtle, Ruby, Rachael, Rodney, and Marie. This family home always impressed me with its simple and plain lines. One would just know the love and tender family care that was inside the doors.

Property 54

We continue west on West Ox Road to the Vernon and Florence Kidwell home. The lot was small, as was the house, which was a one-story, frame construction facing West Ox Road. Mr. Kidwell was employed as a school bus driver for Fairfax County. His run was from Pender to Fairfax Elementary School and to Merrifield, and return to Fairfax Elementary morning and evening. After 1932, the Merrifield run may have been discontinued and the morning and afternoon included a run to the old Oakton High School from Fairfax. As I recall, during the 11 years I was in school, Fairfax County did not provide transportation to old Oakton High School. Only after my freshman year was transportation provided. I never knew any student who rode Mr. Kidwell's bus who did not like and respect him. He looked out for us. He would not leave us. If we were not out on the road, he would stop, blow the horn, and wait until we made it. Tears fill my eyes as I write this. Mr. Kidwell, there are so many of us who would like to ride with you again.

Property 54A

Another property on West Ox Road was owned by Mr. and Mrs. Martin. This couple was in the upper bracket in age. I cannot remember their first names, the size of this property, or much about their home. The Virginia State Forest Service erected a fire tower over 100 feet tall on this property. This structure was removed when Fairfax County's growth made use of the tower obsolete.

Property 54B

The only other property on West Ox Road with which I am familiar enough to discuss was owned by Benjamin C. and Aline A. Fleming. This couple was very active in the Pender Methodist Church. My thoughts tell me Mr. Fleming worked for the U.S. Department of Agriculture and Mrs. Fleming was a schoolteacher in the Fairfax County school system. This property size and the house, other than frame in construction, I cannot recall. This same lack of memory applies to the rest of West Ox Road. It has been too long and I am unable to recall.

Property 37

This was the location of the George and Dorothy Byrne home. This home was of brick construction and Cape Cod in design. The lot size could not have been over an acre. It had a good east view. Mr. Byrne worked as a carpenter and, in later life, dealt in real estate. The Byrnes had one daughter, Betty Jane, who married Clark Dodson. This property is part of the commercial development in the old Pender area.

Property 38

This was the location of the Joe Croson property and home. Mr. Croson ran a store and barber shop on the north side of Little River Turnpike near the intersection of West Ox Road. Mr. Croson was a very talented fiddle or violin player. Mr. and Mrs. Croson were the parents of three children: Roy, Bernice, and Serena. This property, as well as the store, is included in the commercial development and the highway interchange in the old Pender area.

Property 39

This was the location of the Flavius M., 1865-1948, and Frankie Fox, 1866-1944, Allder home. Mr. Allder worked, during the period I knew him, as a finish carpenter on stairways and cabinetry. The Allder family was active in the Pender Methodist Church. Prior to the establishment of the Pender church, Mr. Allder was active in Methodist church work at Jermantown. Family members consisted of Marshall, Madeline, Paul, Roy, Flavius, and Agnes. During World War II, son Flavius B. Allder lost his life. Daughter Agnes Allder graduated from the old Oakton High School in the class of 1924. Today, one might wonder why I keep telling about the people who graduated from the old Oakton High School. Because Fairfax County did not furnish transportation and the distance to high school was more than five miles, it was not an easy task to secure a high school education.

Property 40

This was the location of the Edgar T. and Addie M. Rollins home. Mr. Rollins was employed as a section foreman by the Virginia Department of Highways. The Rollins family had two children, a son, Thomas, and a daughter, Estelle, who also graduated from the old Oakton High School, class of 1931. This home and property are included in the commercial area of the old Pender section of Fairfax County.

Property 41

This was the location of the Ray and Bessie Gooding home and property now in the commercial section of old Pender. Mrs. Bessie Gooding was the official registrar of voters for the Pender precinct. She was also very active in the Pender Methodist Church. Mr. Gooding was employed by the Virginia Department of Highways. The house has been removed and the property is included in this commercial area.

Property 42

This was the location of the Ballard farm and home. My knowledge of the farm size is unknown, as I never visited the home site. Mrs. Maggie

Ballard Allbright drove a Model T Ford car and I would see her driving in the area. The Battle of Ox Hill, which occurred during the Civil War, was fought on this farm on September 1, 1862. This is the location of the only major battle of the Civil War fought in Fairfax County. My thoughts, if they amount to anything, on this subject need not be expressed here. The farm is covered in housing today.

10.2 Location 43, the Civil War monuments to Union generals Kearny and Stevens, who were killed in the Battle of Ox Hill.

10.3 Location 43, rededication of the Kearny and Stevens monuments, 1961.

CHAPTER 10   *Pender*

10.4   Location 43, Fairfax Towne Center shopping center, general area of the Battle of Ox Hill.
Photograph by Vincent Sutphin

10.5   Location 43, Fairfax Towne Center shopping center, general area of the Battle of Ox Hill.
Photograph by Vincent Sutphin

Location 43

This is the location of the Kearney and Stevens memorial, dedicated to two Union generals killed during the Battle of Ox Hill. History of this monument, when and how it was erected, has been well covered by others. During 1961, a rededication of these monuments was held, which my daughter, Linda Ann, and I attended. This was a very impressive ceremony.

Location 44

This was the location of the William and Madeline Cross home and property on the old Legato Road, now abandoned. Mr. Cross worked as a carpenter and also did some light farming. This property no longer exists, having been absorbed in roads and commercial areas. The known family members of the Cross family are: Wallace, Nell, Barbara, and William. Any other members, I am unable to recall.

Property 46A

This is said to be the former location of Aunt Melinda Payne's house. This lady had passed on before my time. This lady was a freed black who had one son by the name of Washington. The size of the property and house description are unknown. In my time, during the 1930s, the property was a storage lot for pulpwood ready to be shipped. When this enterprise was ended, the lot was vacant. The property today is in the West Ox Road/Route 50 interchange.

CHAPTER 10 *Pender*

10.6 **Property 47,** Joe Croson Store and Barber Shop on Route 50, 1960.
Photograph by Vincent Sutphin

10.7 **Property 47,** Route 50 looking east, near the old location of the Joe Croson Store and Barber Shop.
Courtesy of Mrs. Shirley Vanvleet

Nothing Remains the Same   **119**

Property 47

This was the location of the Joe Croson store. It was not a big, impressive building, but a small frame building with a front porch; its location was close to the traveled portion of Route 50. Many tales have been told about the front porch. After some Saturday night events in the area, calls of distress may have been heard coming from the front porch. On investigation one might find a male nailed to the porch floor. The nails were driven through the unfortunate person's clothing, spread-eagled on the porch floor. This and other tales were told to me as a child. Today, I pass on these tales, true or not.

Property 48

The next property was owned by Ralph Croson and his wife. This property was 2 or more acres with a frame, bungalow home. Mr. Croson made his living by transporting milk from local dairy farms to the local dairies in Washington. On the return trip home, he would haul ice and deliver same to customers. He also did other hauling for customers. The known Croson children were Welby, Louise, and Louellen.

Property 49

The property next along the highway was owned by Jim Thompson and his wife. This property contained a small, frame, bungalow-type house, painted, and well-kept. Mr. Thompson, during the 1930s, had a small store and gas station built. He sold Amoco gas and oil. Mr. Thompson also owned and operated a dump truck for the Virginia Department of Highways. I am unable to recall the Thompson children or the estimated size of their property.

Property 50

During the early 1950s, Welby Croson and his wife owned the next property. The size is unknown and the house on this lot was of frame and not large. Mr. Croson attended elementary school with me. Due to the early death of his father, he had to quit school and involve himself in the milk route and ice-delivery business of the family. As time progressed,

CHAPTER 10 *Pender*

he drove a delivery truck for others. Today this whole area is commercial and no houses remain in the old Pender area.

Property 51

Between Little River Turnpike, Route 50, West Ox Road, and Route 608, the Virginia Department of Forestry erected a fire tower during the 1930s. This tower's height must have been close to 100 feet, as land elevation in the Pender area was over 500 feet, and the view from this tower was outstanding in all directions. During the spring and fall, this tower would be manned. After Pearl Harbor, the United States Army had a small detachment assigned to this duty for air raid spotting. The length of time the army performed this duty is unknown because I soon found myself on duty at Fort Knox, Kentucky. When this tower was removed, I do not recall.

10.8 Property 52, Fair Oaks District Police Station and Fair Oaks Fire Station 21, on the site of the Piney Ridge farm. The old Navy Volunteer Fire Department moved into this building when it was first constructed.

Nothing Remains the Same **121**

10.9 Property 52, Christ Presbyterian Church, on the site of the Piney Ridge farm.

10.10 Property 52, Pender United Methodist Church, on the site of the Piney Ridge farm.

Property 52

Piney Ridge Farm is next on our list. The owners of this farm before the Civil War were Charles and Eleanor Stewart. This couple moved to the Pender area from New York. This couple had one son, Charles Lewis, 1826-1927, who married Fannie Gibson, for his first wife, and Henrietta V. Howard for his second wife. This couple had two children, Norman H. and Fannie. Norman H. married Mamie Twombly, and Fannie married Lyman H. Bryce. Charles Lewis fought in the Civil War for the Confederate Army. Mosby was active in this area, as were some units of the 15th Virginia Cavalry. No application for Confederate pension has been mentioned. The house on this farm was a large, two-story, painted, frame one with a full front porch. The house was given to Fairfax County and moved across the highway to Dorforth Drive. The house was allowed to deteriorate and was destroyed. The street has been closed. The only family whom I knew to occupy this home was the E.F. Stowe family, whose ownership was before 1925 to at least the 1940s. This family had two sons, Alfred and Robert. After the old Pender School was closed, they attended school in Fairfax. I think they finished high school in Herndon. I have no intention of getting in any discussion on the Battle of Ox Hill, or the locations of General Headquarters, or what after-battle action may or may not have taken place. The best and most complete explanation I have read was written by Lt. Col. Robert Ross Smith, USAR, in 1961 in an article republished by the Fairfax County Board of Supervisors in the book *Fairfax County and the War Between the States.* The farm is now covered with a police and fire station, commercial buildings, and Dominion Electric Power sub-station. The large building owned by the power company has been sold, and will be converted into a large church operation at some future date. The next adjoining property contains two churches facing Little River Turnpike (Route 50). They are Christ Presbyterian Church and Pender Methodist Church. We are now at Fairfax County Parkway, which ends my discussion on the old Pender community.

Chapter 11

Legato – South Side of Warrenton Pike

Property 147

Difficult Run passes under the Warrenton Pike (also known as Lee Highway or the 29th Division Highway or Route 29) at this point. This was the beginning of the Legato area.

11.1 Property 148 on the right, Properties 113 and 114, discussed in Chapter 12, on the left. This is the Legato area, starting at Lee Highway and Village Drive. The property on the right was the location of the old Mills farm, owned by members of the Swart family. The Swarts also owned Property 113 on the left. The Mills farm on the right is now occupied by a State Farm Insurance office, a former auto transmission shop to be replaced with a bank, and an auto repair shop. Properties 113 and 114 on the left are now occupied by apartment buildings and a Wegmans grocery store.

CHAPTER 11   *Legato – South Side of Warrenton Pike*

11.2 Property 148, Village Drive and Lee Highway. This building is to be replaced with a bank building.

11.3 Property 148, the State Farm Insurance Company building at Village Drive and Lee Highway.

Property 148

This was the location of the old Mills farm. This farm was owned by the John Henry Swart family. The farm was sold during the 1950s and developed as Lee High Village subdivision. This subdivision contained many houses and, at one time, had a number of undeveloped lots. Most of these lots today have large, expensive homes on them. Three large commercial buildings are at the Lee Highway entrance to the subdivision. One of these buildings is to be replaced with a bank on the west corner.

Property 149

This was the location of the former Charles Woodrick, Miller Kielsgard, Dunbar home and property. Today this property is covered with at least 25 large and expensive homes with an entrance off Arniel Place, which is off a service road from Village Drive. At the west end of the service road are the remains of an unfinished, pre-Civil War railroad bed. Other owners of this property, I am unable to recall. After World War II, one was an automobile dealership. The next was a tree and yard business. This is the limit of my ability to recall.

Property 150

McKinsey Avenue intersects with Warrenton Pike at this point, and runs 1,500 to 2,000 feet to the south. This is a narrow, undeveloped, and ungraded outlet road. On its east side, about 600 feet off Warrenton Pike, is located a large family cemetery. This cemetery is known as the Kidwell-Robertson Family Cemetery. Many graves are marked, and the cemetery is well kept.

Property 151

This was the location of the old Marshall Allder and Mary Robertson Allder home and property. The family had two daughters, Dorothy Allder Rhodes, who is deceased, and Alice Allder Burleson, who occupies the family home today. The size of this property is unknown.

CHAPTER 11   *Legato – South Side of Warrenton Pike*

The Marshall Allder family may be interred in the family graveyard, Kidwell-Robertson, which is nearby.

Property 151A

This was the location of a large farm known as the Robertson farm. John and Elliott Robertson lived on this farm, which I have been told contained more than 157 acres. The entrance to this property was by McKinsey Avenue, past the Marshall Allder home from Lee Highway (Route 29). Today the property is covered with large, expensive homes and an entrance to the subdivision. McKinsey Avenue is no longer used. Both Elliott and John Robertson are interred in the family cemetery on McKinsey Avenue. My personal knowledge of this farm was limited, and this information has been obtained from Mrs. Marvin O. Seek, the former Kathleen Robertson, daughter of Earnest and Minnie K. Robertson. Earnest Robertson was a brother of Elliott and John.

11.4   Property 153, shopping area located off of Lee Highway on the old Robertson farm. This is the site of the old Manuel Tourist Court and Restaurant.

Nothing Remains the Same

Property 153

This was the location of the old Manuel Tourist Court and Restaurant and gas station. The dwelling house for the Manuel family and at least one other dwelling, which was rented, were located on this property. Mr. and Mrs. Manuel did business at this location for a period of more than 15 years before moving from the area. Frank White ran the restaurant for a period of time. I am not familiar with the status of the tourist court during that period. Today this whole area is occupied by a modern-type, commercial shopping center.

Property 154

This was the location of a small dwelling, and the size of this property is unknown. This property changed owners several times and memory does not help me. Today, this property is occupied by a subdivision with large, expensive housing, or is part of the previously discussed shopping area.

Property 155

This was the location of a brick Cape Cod house occupied by Marvin O. Seek and his wife, Kathleen R. Seek. Mrs. Seek taught for a number of years in the Fairfax County School system. Mr. Seek was in the well drilling and construction business in Fairfax County. Their house and property were sold. This couple moved from the area, and large, expensive housing now covers their former homestead. Mrs. Seek gave me the information on her father's family and the Kline family, as well as other information on the Legato area, which made life much easier for me in my attempt to tell these stories.

Property 156

This was the location of the property formerly owned by Mr. and Mrs. Earnest Robertson. This property is now part of the previously-mentioned subdivision of large, expensive homes. At one time, Mr. and Mrs. Earnest Robertson's property consisted of more than 20 acres fronting on Lee Highway. By time of the subdivision development, sale of this property to others had reduced its size. Mr. Earnest Robertson married Minnie Kline. They were the parents of Kathleen R. Seek, as previously mentioned.

11.5 Property 157. During the 1930s-1940s this was Mr. Charlie Kline's General Store. It is now occupied as an antique shop and furniture and rug store.

Property 156A

This piece of property was brought to my attention by Mrs. Kathleen Seek. It contained 10 acres and was owned by her uncle, George Robertson. Today this property is also part of the previously-mentioned subdivision containing large, expensive homes.

Property 157

This was the location of the Charlie and Annie J. Kline home. The Kline property contained 7 acres more or less. The Klines purchased this property during the 1930s after moving back to this area from Manassas. They had a small house built back from the highway, and a small store built near the highway. Mr. Kline operated this store for a number of years. I am not clear when the Klines passed away, but I know they are interred at Oakton United Brethren Church Cemetery. The store building is now an antique shop, and also sells rugs and furniture. The house is used as a dwelling. The current ownership of this and the store property is unknown.

Property 158

Several houses facing Lee Highway were built by Graham Russell, Mr. Kline's son-in-law, during the 1930s, and sold. Who purchased these homes and their present ownership is unknown by me.

Property 158A

During the 1930s and early 1940s, Gladys Winfield developed and sold lots in a subdivision known as Glen Alden. This subdivision consisted of two streets. The first we come to that intersects with Lee Highway is Holly Avenue. This street is about one-half mile long, and runs in a southern direction off Lee Highway. It contains 22 houses on both its east and west side. These houses are of all periods of construction; small, medium, and large in size; and expensive. Ownership of these houses is unknown, as several are unoccupied, and several lots contain new housing under construction. Facing Lee Highway is a small store on the northwest corner of Holly Avenue. Between the store (which is occupied as a business) and Spruce Avenue are two small houses which face Lee Highway, and are occupied by unknown parties. We come to Spruce Avenue, which contains 27 homes, which are large, expensive homes. Both streets are paved, with no curb or gutters, not much grading or drainage, and very little parking space. Ownership of these properties is unknown. This explanation covers what I know of the Glen Alden subdivision today and in the past.

Property 158B

On the northwest corner of Spruce Avenue is a large, modern building, which houses childcare. This building faces Lee Highway, with a service entrance from the highway at Marymead Drive.

CHAPTER 11   *Legato – South Side of Warrenton Pike*

Property 158C

Today a frame bungalow occupies about 5 acres, and is a private dwelling with a horse barn and two horses. During the 1940s this house was occupied by a family by the name of Isdell with two daughters, Mary and Dottie. My knowledge of this family and the property size is limited. My memory thinks that most of this property today is covered in a subdivision called Marymead. The entrance to this subdivision is through Marymead Drive, which intersects with Lee Highway. The bungalow faces Lee Highway with a service road entrance. This service entrance also connects with Marymead Drive at the Lee Highway intersection. Along Marymead Drive, into the subdivision on its east and west sides are 24 expensive homes. Ownerships are unknown. I wish to express my appreciation to Gwen Beck who donated her time to help me field check Properties 158A through 158C. Thank you very much, or this would never have occurred in such detail.

Property 159

Two houses facing Lee Highway, with entrances off the previously-mentioned service road connecting to Marymead Drive, were built in the late 1930s or early 1940s. Ownership then, as well as today, is unknown.

11.6 Property 160, Merrifield Garden Center. This building is located on or near the old Sisson distillery building on Lee Highway, across from the old Jake Russell Store.

Nothing Remains the Same

Property 160

The Sisson distillery occupied the next property. This included a two-story, frame dwelling. It is my understanding that this distillery operated before Prohibition. It has been told that the Sissons also operated a store from this building. My father rode a horse from Fairfax Station and had a back tooth extracted at the distillery by a Mr. Bob Sisson, who owned a set of tooth extraction tools. The main building size was approximately 40 by 30 feet, of stone construction, at least 20 feet tall, with a hipped roof. The period I am discussing here is from the late 1910s until the building was removed. During this period, a Mr. Smith occupied the frame house. He raised garden plants and sold garden products such as corn, beans, potatoes, and other in-season produce. During this period, the main building was occupied as an auto repair shop. As to additional information, I checked with Gladys Sisson Potterton, who was unable to help me. Additional checking with Lee Hubbard helped me as to ownership. The owners were Elhannon B. and Nannie Hersey Sisson. Mr. Sisson was a Confederate veteran who died October 23, 1914, and is interred in Fairfax Cemetery. This information was obtained from *The Fairfax Herald* newspaper. The Sisson couple's house was located on the north side of Lee Highway, as previously mentioned by me. During my time this property was occupied by two daughters, Rosa and Viola, known as the Sisson ladies. Mayo and Connie Stuntz have printed a book depicting the glass negatives of "The Rambler," J. Harry Shannon. Page 266 shows the east view of the distillery from Warrenton Pike. Piney Branch headwaters rise with fresh spring water across the road from this location, and pass through the distillery location. My hopes are high that the little I may have recalled, and what others have helped me with, will benefit someone. Today, Merrifield Gardens covers most of what may have been distillery property. Two modern homes with an entrance from a service road are on the property between Merrifield Gardens and Piney Branch Road.

Property 161

Piney Branch Road, during my time, was a dirt road less than 30 feet wide that ran south of Lee Highway for less than half a mile. The only

CHAPTER 11   *Legato – South Side of Warrenton Pike*

home I can remember was occupied by Sam Lightfoot and his wife and family. The family home was on the left, or east, side. On the right, or west, side of the road was a small family cemetery of the Millan family. This would be about the extent of my travel on this road, and I would turn around as the road dead-ended. Today this road connects with Pheasant Ridge Road, and provides the main entrance road for 10 to 15 large, expensive homes.

Property 162
At the west corner of Piney Branch and Warrenton Pike (Route 29) was a large, very impressive, frame home. This was occupied by a family by the name of Woodward. The house was removed and the property developed and a new house built. Owners and developers are unknown.

Property 163
The next property contained a small house, lot size is unknown. The house has been removed. The property appears to be included in the Route 29/Fairfax County Parkway (Route 7100) interchange.

Property 164
This was the location of the Major and Lutie Robey property. Mr. Robey worked as a blacksmith for the Virginia Department of Highways for a number of years. His income was supplemented by the raising and selling of vegetables from the large garden he tended. Mrs. Robey, my aunt, also supplemented their income as a cook at the old Hunters Lodge and Dance Hall across the highway from the Robey home. Her other activities were doing laundry and quilting. The Robey property was sold during the 1960s, and they moved to the Thoroughfare Gap area.

Property 165
This was the location of the old Legato school property. This building, after the school was closed, was used as a dwelling. Fairfax County acquired the old building, had it moved to the courthouse lot at Fairfax,

11.7 Property 165, the old Legato School as a dwelling in its original location.
Photograph by Lee Hubbard, ca. 1969

and had the building restored as a one-room school museum for the public to view. Three previously-mentioned schoolteachers were Leo Haines, Miss Lillian Millan, and Miss Mary Millan.

Property 166

This was the location of the Buckley Baptist Chapel of the Old School Baptist Church. This property was acquired from the Buckley family. As I recall, this church was still in operation during the late 1920s. At some later date, during the 1930s, Gladys Winfield gained ownership of the building and property, and converted the building into a house. Other ownership of the building and property, I am unable to recall. Today the building has been removed.

Property 166A

This is the location of the Fairfax County Parkway (Route 7100) and Route 29 interchange.

CHAPTER 11   *Legato – South Side of Warrenton Pike*

11.8 Property 166B, the Alexander and Mary Ann Buckley dwelling. Information on this property from Mrs. Claudette Crouch Ward.
Photograph by Vincent Sutphin

11.9 Property 166B, the Alexander and Mary Ann Buckley dwelling. Information on this property from Mrs. Claudette Crouch Ward.
Photograph by Vincent Sutphin

11.10 Property 166B, the Alexander and Mary Ann Buckley dwelling. Information on this property from Mrs. Claudette Crouch Ward.
Photograph by Vincent Sutphin

11.11 Property 166B, the Alexander and Mary Ann Buckley dwelling. Information on this property from Mrs. Claudette Crouch Ward.
Photograph by Vincent Sutphin

CHAPTER 11   *Legato – South Side of Warrenton Pike*

Property 166B

The next property I wish to discuss must be visited through Cannon Ridge subdivision. This was one of the enjoyable sights of Fairfax County; however, it is now private property. The house I am discussing was once owned by Alexander Buckley and his wife, Mary Ann. The opportunity to visit this house has only occurred to me twice, so my knowledge is limited. The house has two stories. The original house is of log construction, with a private outlet road about one-half mile long. My source of information is Mrs. Claudette Crouch Ward, whose grandfather and grandmother, Norman and Abbie Buckley Crouch, lived here for over 25 years after their marriage, when the property was owned by the Alexander and Mary Ann Buckley descendants. During that period, this property contained about 187 acres.

Property 167

This was the location of a former house, now a business called My Home Shop, 12501 Lee Highway. The owner is unknown.

11.12 Property 168, Betty's Azalea Ranch, located on a service road along Lee Highway.

Property 168

This is the location of Betty's Azalea Ranch. The owner is now unknown. It is operating as a plant nursery business.

11.13 Property 169, Rustic Glen, former home of Judge and Mrs. Hazel Ferguson, relocated and under renovation. The property is now owned by their daughter, Evelyn F. Lancaster. Property information furnished by Lee Hubbard and Jack Q. Spitler.
Photographing permission from Jack Q. Spitler, Jr.; photograph by Vincent Sutphin

11.14 Property 169, Rustic Glen.
Photographing permission from Jack Q. Spitler, Jr.; photograph by Vincent Sutphin

12.1 Property 113 and part

CHAPTER 11   *Legato – South Side of Warrenton Pike*

Property 169

Hazel Ferguson Drive is a new street with newly constructed, large, expensive houses. Ownership of these homes is unknown. Before the Civil War, this property was owned by William and Lizzie Berkley, containing a private cemetery. Several members of the Berkley family were interred here, as well as members of the Taylor family. During the 1940s, Judge and Mrs. Hazel Ferguson owned this property. It is thought that as long as Judge and Mrs. Ferguson owned the property, the family cemetery stones remained. The judge was well known in the Arlington County Court system.

Property 170

We return to the service road, traveling west. We pass in front of five modern homes, and come to Summit Drive. Crossing Summit Drive, the service road ends, providing an outlet for two more houses. Summit Drive is the main outlet to this large subdivision, called Crystal Springs, with numerous large, expensive, and well-kept homes. This concludes what I can remember of the south side of Warrenton Pike, Route 29, in the Legato area. We must return now to the point of beginning to try to remember what was on the north side of this Virginia highway.

Chapter 12

Legato – North Side of Warrenton Pike

of Property 114, Wegmans grocery store in the Legato area at the corner of Route 29 and Monument Drive

12.2 Property 118,

Property 113

This was the location of the Tom Harrison home and property. The size of the property is unknown. Tom Harrison was a Civil War veteran and an uncle of Rose J. Haines. I can no longer recall the date of Mr. Harrison's death. The property and house were acquired by Walter Lehman. After becoming the owner of this property and adding several tourist cabins, Mr. Lehman opened a tavern. This must have been later than 1933, because the sale of beer would not have been legal. Mr. Lehman was an immigrant from Germany, and during the 1940s testified before Congress on several occasions on subjects pertaining to the new German government. The old tavern is gone and the new Wegmans groceries store and parking lot now occupy this location.

Property 114

This was the location of a large, wooded tract of property containing approximately 118 acres and owned by the members of the John H. Swart family. Today this property is occupied by a large housing project.

Property 115

This was the location of the old Glen Myers, Gus Burke, and Bloomer and Frank White property and home. This was a big piece of property and, during the 1920s, was farmed. I am unable to give many details as to the farm size or the type of housing there. Today this property is covered with housing of different types, as well as streets and parking lots.

Property 116

This was the location of a good-size, frame house. This was a typical farmhouse and the old farm was known as the Gooding farm. During the 1930s, this home was occupied by the Newman family. Family members were Adrian, Benjamin, William, and twin daughters, America and Frances. Today, this property is occupied by streets, parking lots, and housing.

Property 117

This was the location of the Sisson family home. In my time, two Sisson ladies, Rose and Viola, lived in a two-story, frame home set back several hundred feet from the highway on a slight rise which was several feet higher than the roadbed. The Sisson family operated a distillery in the Legato area before Prohibition. This operation was carried on in a large stone building across the road from the Legato store, on a small stream. This is the lot where Merrifield Gardens now runs a nursery. The Sisson home and property are now occupied as a townhouse development.

the Wesley Swart family home, located at Lee Highway and Legato Road (demolished).

12.3 Property 118, the Wesley

Swart family home, located at Lee Highway and Legato Road (demolished).

12.4 Property 118, Fairfax

CHAPTER 12   *Legato –North Side of Warrenton Pike*

County Fire Station 40, located on the Wesley Swart property at Lee Highway and Legato Road.
12.5 Property 120, the

Property 118

This was the location of the Wesley Swart and Lula May Gooding home and farm. The Swarts were the parents of two daughters, Myrtle, who married Roy Allder, and Edna May, who married Paul F. Allder. Today the property is occupied by the Fairfax County Fire and Rescue Station #40.

Property 119

For a few years, Gus Burke operated a dairy farm, which was sold to Alice Haines. She turned the farm into a poultry and egg business. Alice Haines operated this farm with male help, as she was blind. Eleanor Roosevelt was a frequent visitor to the farm, as she is said to have been a personal friend of Alice Haines. This property was located on the west side of Legato Road and is now covered with housing projects.

Property 120

This was the location of a general store operated by H.M.F. Palmer and then by Jake Russell. This store no longer exists.

former Palmer store, with the Wesley Swart home, Property 118, in the distance. In later years, Jake Russell operated the store. Today, the property is unoccupied.

Property 121

This was the location of a home once occupied by the H.M.F. Palmer family. The Palmer family left the area during the late 1930s. The house is gone now.

Property 122

This was the location of the John and Carrie Thompson Crouch family home. Mr. and Mrs. Crouch were the parents of Myrtle, John Leo, Lorraine, and Wilton Lee Crouch. Mrs. Crouch died from the result of being struck by an automobile while crossing the highway near their home. The house on this property was two-story and frame. Mr. Crouch was employed by the Virginia Department of Highways. The house is no longer standing. The property was included in the housing project and other developments in this general area.

Property 123

The next property, which was developed after 1945, was the Dinner

Bell Restaurant. The owner of this property and the small building is unknown. While this restaurant was not nationally known, the place was clean, the food was reasonably priced and good. Like everything else in the area, it, too, is gone.

Property 124

The major attraction in this area after 1945 was "Virginia City." This was a western-type amusement park, featuring street gunfights, cowboys, costumed Indians, stagecoaches, and other entertainment, including dancing ladies, gambling, and card-playing men. The building faced a dirt street. Some business had false fronts with a cattle-town background, including dance halls and make-believe saloons. Parents brought their children and they saw a show. Today this is all gone. We have an intersection with stoplights and overpasses where the traffic does not have to stop.

12.6 Property 125, the old Hunters Lodge and Dance Hall, located on Lee Highway at West Ox Road. It is no longer standing.

Property 125

This was the location of the old Hunters Lodge Night Club and Dance Hall. This building was built of logs, slab lumber, and other materials. It was no higher than 15 feet tall. It had a large fireplace and chimney of stone and brick. The dance floor was oak. This place of entertainment opened during the 1930s and the closing date must have been in the 1980s. Like all other properties in the area, it became commercial property, or part of Fairfax County Parkway, or the interchange with Route 29.

Property 124A

This was the location of the old 29 Drive-In Theater. It was located on the east side of West Ox Road in the rear of Hunters' Lodge. Like all the rest, it, too, is gone and now commercial property.

Property 124B

This was the location of the old Millan home and farm tenant house. The main Millan house was a large two-story farm dwelling of frame construction. During the early 1930s, on a dirt road, there once stood a marker relating this family's activities during the Revolutionary War, as well as J.E.B. Stewart's activities during the Civil War. This marker disappeared during the 1930s and was never replaced. Miss Mary and Miss Lillian were Fairfax County schoolteachers. They both taught at Jermantown and Legato schools. The Millan property is now occupied by the Virginia State Highway Department's shop and maintenance facilities, Fairfax County Sanitation and Waste, a fire training station, and Route 66 on the north side. Across West Ox Road, along its east side from Lee Highway to Route 66, are commercial buildings. The Fair Oaks Church now occupies this property.

Property 126

Facing Route 29, at the Route 608 intersection, was the home of Joseph Buckley. This was a two-story, frame home, well kept up, and painted. It

CHAPTER 12   *Legato –North Side of Warrenton Pike*

was located on a good-size piece of cleared land. This home, as most of the property, is now owned by Fairfax County, or is under development by Fairfax County for its use.

Property 127

A Fairfax family owned property and a house in this area. Due to so many changes, and the Fairfax County Parkway, I am unable to come up with a location.

Property 128

The next property was owned by the John Buckley family. Two Buckley family homes faced Route 29 with a rear entrance from a street in the back. This was a large piece of property that has been developed into a very attractive housing development.

12.7   Property 128A, formerly the old Happy Hour Dance Hall. The building still stands and is operated as a tool rental business.

Nothing Remains the Same

12.8 Property 128A, formerly the old Happy Hour Dance Hall. This was the first dance hall built in the Centreville/Legato area. It was owned and operated by the Mohr family.

Property 128A

This is the location of the old Happy Hour Dance Hall. This is a large building, one-story, and still standing today. This dance hall operated on Friday and Saturday nights. Live country music was played, and the dance hall was said to have the best oak dance floor in Northern Virginia. Soft drinks, beer, and light snacks were sold. The music was great; so were the dancers. This dance hall was owned and operated by the Mohrs, a German family in middle age. On several occasions, these dance halls were visited by me. I cannot recall too many disturbances or misbehavior that amounted to anything before it was broken up by bouncers. These places of entertainment were all visited by the Fairfax County Sheriff's Department and later by the police, when the Fairfax County Police Force was organized. The Mohr family lived about a half mile north of the dance hall in a small house, until their deaths. The dance hall stands today, and houses an equipment rental business.

Property 128B

The Armand family lived in a frame house along what was termed a dirt road. I never visited their house. This family was said to be German, and was in the wood business during the late 1930s. When Pender Methodist Church was first organized, several Armand family members were listed as members.

CHAPTER 12 *Legato –North Side of Warrenton Pike*

12.9 Property 128C, Briarwood Manor, home of Edith Thompson, built in the 1930s. Edith Thompson was well known in Fairfax County as a teacher and elementary school supervisor.

Property 128C

Edith Thompson, a former Fairfax County schoolteacher and elementary school supervisor, who also owned and operated her own private school, had a large and impressive home built at this location during the 1930s, which she named Briarwood Manor. The size of this property and other family details are unknown by me. This will end what I can remember of the Legato area. I am not as well versed in this area as I am in the other areas discussed. The area, in my time, had more individual homes, and property seemed to be of smaller size and more populated. I did not often visit this area.

Chapter 13

Waples Mill Community

Waples Mill Road connects to Route 50 in the Route 50/Route 66 interchange in the Jermantown area. This has always been true. Where the Waples Mill community started and where the Jermantown community ended, there was no natural boundary. With the construction of Route 66, I will make one. It will begin on the west side of Route 66, starting at the overhead bridge on Waples Mill Road and traveling north and west on Waples Mill Road toward the pre-Civil War community of Fox Mill, now known as Waples Mill, then along Fox Mill Road toward the Vale community for about a mile. Turn around and return to Waples Mill Road, then travel west along Waples Mill Road for about one-and-one-half miles towards the Navy community, then travel east on Oakton Road at its intersection with Waples Mill Road to Jermantown Road for over a mile. This area is what I will discuss as the Waples Mill community as I knew it as a boy, a teenager, a young man, and, with the best of my ability, to write from memory as an old man. Fox Mill Road begins at the Waples Mill community at the Difficult Run Bridge and runs past the old Fox Mill location, continuing through to the community of Vale, through to Moneys Corner, and to its termination with Centreville Road south of Herndon. Waples Mill Road continues west to its connection with Route 608 southeast of the community of Navy. In the past, these two roads were a means of travel to Herndon, Floris, Navy, and Leesburg, or any point northwest, in addition to their connection to the two mills previously mentioned. Anyone using these two roads in the past had to take into consideration road conditions, because in the wintertime, travel would be limited to local conditions only. Today, one is limited to a very moderate rate of speed. These roads both maintain about the same uphill and downhill grade as they did more than a hundred years ago, and in driving, care must be observed. We begin with the John E. and Lucy Jackson family, who owned this piece of property in the 1920s and 1930s. During that period of time on the west end of the property was a two-story, frame, unfinished house. This house burned in the early morning in the 1930s; the cause was unknown. This property is now part of a developed subdivision containing from six to eight houses, which is completed along the Valley Road and Michelle Court.

CHAPTER 13   *Waples Mill Community*

Property 217

The next property on the east side of Waples Mill Road was owned by O.J. Collins and his wife. Acreage is unknown. For a number of years, Mr. Collins was employed by Russell Haines in the huckster business, and later by the Virginia Department of Highways. This employment probably continued until Mr. Collins was no longer able to work. The Collins' home was a large two-story, frame house, probably containing five or more rooms. Mr. and Mrs. Collins sold several acres on the rear of the property to Mr. and Mrs. Paul Rice. Mr. Rice was another state highway employee.

Property 218

Mr. Paul Rice and wife, Rosa Lee, built their frame home on the property they purchased from O. J. Collins. Mr. Rice was employed by the Virginia Department of Highways. The Rice family was also active in the Pender Methodist Church, including their daughter, Eugenia, and son, Paul Lee. Today, what was the Rice outlet road is Derosnec Drive, and what was the Rice and O.J. Collins property contains nine large, expensive, brick homes.

Property 219

The next property contained 3 acres and was owned by Arvine and Minnie Chinn Wells. This property sat on a knoll some 10 feet above Waples Mill Road, on which the Wells built their frame, one-story home. Mr. Wells was employed by the United States Agriculture Department for a number of years. Mr. and Mrs. Wells were the parents of one daughter, Jacqueline. The Wells' family acquired the John Chinn farm after Mr. Chinn's death in 1936.

Property 220

The adjoining property on the northeast side of Waples Mill Road was owned by Lou Hall and his wife, Jenny. Mr. Hall died during the 1930s and the property was unoccupied for a number of years. The house burned in about 1935, cause unknown. This property was wooded and

Nothing Remains the Same   **157**

had a steep entrance, as it, too, sat some 10 feet above the roadbed. Mrs. Jenny Hall worked as a domestic, keeping house for other families, and did not occupy the property after her husband's death. This property may be included in the 3 acres which the Wells' acquired to build their house as I discussed in Property 219.

Property 221

The next property was wooded. The number of acres is unknown, and the land was higher than the roadbed by 10 to 12 feet. During the late 1930s, the Greenstreet family acquired this property, and built a large, two-story, frame house there. Members of the Greenstreet family were believed to have been employed by the United States government. The house built by the Greenstreet family is still present on this property. Present ownership is unknown. The Greenstreet property ran along a small stream on the north to the intersection of Waples Mill Road and Oakton Road.

Property 222

This brings us to the crossing of a small stream from the Jermantown area and the intersection of Waples Mill Road and what is now Oakton Road. We will continue to reminisce on the north side of Waples Mill Road, and pick up any connecting roads along the way. At this intersection, on the north side of Waples Mill Road and Oakton Road, stood a small, frame house in 1932. This house was occupied by two men. Their names and occupations were unknown. One was about 20 years old, and the other was about 40. He drove a new 1932 Ford Model B car. Gasoline for the car was purchased at my uncle's general store at Jermantown. This property today is unoccupied and covered with underbrush.

Property 223

Continuing northwest, on the north side of Waples Mill Road was a small, unpainted building. It was said to have been a Dunkard church, 1920 to 1930. I have been told by some that Mrs. Stella Waple Rhodes, a blind lady, played the organ, and her one-armed husband was the preacher at this small church. Services were discontinued here, and I do not remember when the church was torn down. The location is now unoccupied, and the present owner is unknown.

Property 224

Following the Civil War, the property next discussed is believed to have been owned by Thomas and Martha Jane Monroe Lee. The size of this property is unknown. The two-story, frame house overlooked the Chinn farm, upper Difficult Run Valley, Waples Mill Road and Fox Mill Road intersections, and Difficult Run Bridge. Thomas Lee is thought to have been the brother of Ruben M. Lee and brother-in-law of Deskin Monroe, all three Confederate Army veterans. Ruben lost his life at Five Forks, Virginia. During my time, the Lees' property was occupied by George B. and his wife, Annie Waple Lee. George B., as well as Norman, William, Effie M., Marion N., and Lelia were children of Thomas F. and Jane Monroe Lee. George B. and Annie Waple Lee were the parents of George E., Helen B., Fay, Blanche, Bernice, and Walton B. Lee. Another son of Thomas F. and Jane Monroe Lee, William Lee, and Ida B. Wells, his wife, lived in Fairfax. Both he and his brother, George B., worked for the old Arlington & Fairfax Electric Trolley line during its operation in the 1910s up until it closed during the late 1930s. During the period following the Civil War, Thomas F. Lee, his son, George B., as well as Deskin Monroe, all worked as teamsters for my late grandfather, Stephen P. Twombly. Thomas F. Lee is alleged to have died in 1907, and to be interred on his farm at Waples Mill Road. This property was later acquired by two ladies, Nellie T. Martin, and I am unable to supply the other's name. They raised chickens and sold eggs for a number of years. The old house is no longer standing, and the property, as I knew it, was called "The Lees." It is now occupied by numerous large, expensive homes.

13.1 Property 225, site of the Fox Mill dam on Difficult Run.
Photograph by Vincent Sutphin

Property 225

The property between The Lees and Difficult Run consists of low, flat, flood plain and runs along the Difficult Run approximately one-half mile. This property contains what is known as the old High Banks Swimming Hole, as well as the remains of the old Fox Mill Dam, and what appears to be the old Fox Mill location. This mill was burned at the beginning of the Civil War by Union troops, and never rebuilt. This property is discussed in detail in *Yearbook: The Historical Society of Fairfax County, VA, Volume 8, 1962-1963*, in a biography of Sara Summers Clark, written in the first person by Ralph Leroy Millicent. This is an excellent article on the area and old Fox Mill. Present owners of this and other surrounding property are unknown.

Property 226

During the 1930s, a small log house still remained on the west side of Fox Mill Road at the old Fox Mill site. This house was allegedly occupied by the miller before the Civil War burning of the mill. The family who occupied the house during the 1930s was the Burleighs. This family had several boys whom I came to know as swimmers in the previously mentioned High Banks Swimming Hole. One son was employed by Virginia Electric and Power Company during the time

CHAPTER 13   *Waples Mill Community*

13.2   Property 225, Fox Mill millrace looking south on Fox Mill Road, possibly near the location of the old mill.
Photograph by Vincent Sutphin

13.3   Property 225, Fox Mill dam on Difficult Run.
Photograph by Vincent Sutphin

Nothing Remains the Same   **161**

I was also employed there. This was Dewey H. Burleigh, Jr., who is now deceased and missed by me, because we can no longer discuss swimming at High Banks, and other activities. To continue my story, we must return to Waples Mill Road where it crosses Route 66, and pick up the west side at this point.

Property 226A

During the 1920s and 1930s, the major property owners on the west side of Waples Mill Road that I can recall were Oliver F. and Ida M. Hall, and John and Sara Chinn. The Halls' south property line joined the John and Lucy Jackson north property line. The Halls' west property line joined the Neffs', and their north line joined the Chinns'. The east property line ran along Waples Mill Road for approximately one-third of a mile. The Halls sold their property to the Schaefer family, who later sold to Fred Molock. The Hall family also sold property to Harold Johnson and his wife, from whom Warren Robertson and his wife acquired the property after World War II. Who else may have acquired property from the Halls or their heirs is unknown. At least nine houses today occupy what I knew as the Oliver Hall property.

13.4 Property 226B, the John Chinn home, rear view. The home faced Waples Mill Road.
Courtesy of Jackie Puckett

CHAPTER 13   **Waples Mill Community**

13.5   Property 226B, Mr. John Chinn, Confederate veteran.
Courtesy of Paul Sutphin and Jackie Puckett

Property 226B

The next property was owned by the John Chinn family, and joined the Hall and Neff properties to the south, with Waples Mill Road forming the east and north boundaries. Difficult Run formed the west boundary, containing some 57 acres, more or less. The southern section of this property was hilly. The middle section of this farm had a small stream with very fertile land on both sides of the stream until it emptied into Difficult Run. This area was flat, with very good pasture, and grew good crops. The Chinn home was a frame structure with a front porch. Mr. John Chinn was a former Confederate veteran, and blind. During good weather, one would find him sitting in a rocking chair on the front porch. All the property has been sold. The southern part containing the large hill has been developed and now has 16 large homes on the site, with the remaining property in the developmental stage. Members of the Chinn family were Minnie, Dora, Sam, John, Tom, and Charlie. On Mr. Chinn's death during 1936, this property was acquired by his daughter, Minnie, who had married Arvine Wells. Mrs. Wells sold the farm to the developers of Waples Mill Manor, which now contains 16 large homes.

The remaining flood plain property to date is undeveloped. Mr. John Chinn acquired this property from the Alexander family before the 1920s. Mr. John Chinn was a former member of the Confederate Army, and was an active member of the old John Marr Camp of Confederate War veterans. This subdivision is now called Waples Mill Manor. The development of this, as other subdivisions on Waples Mill Road and Oakton Road, contains large houses, but the layout of the streets and the location of the houses on these hilly lots are outstanding.

Vale Community

Today, to write of all this and not mention the Vale Community would be an insult to the community and all my old friends with whom I attended elementary and high school. The only reason I cannot do the same is because I am not familiar enough with the area to do so. At the intersection of Route 665, Fox Mill Road, and Route 671, Hunt Road, on the southwest side in the woods, was a small house and some acres which were owned by a Mrs. Breeden. The only time I visited this property was in 1933 while delivering supplies to Mrs. Breeden from my uncle's store at Jermantown. During the 1940s, Mrs. Breeden's daughter and granddaughter joined her. They all lived in the small house. The Breedens' property is now covered with large and expensive homes. No attempt was made to find out how many, or their ownership.

Along Route 671 (Hunt Road), well set back on a hill, was the home of Mr. Maurice Fox and his wife. The Fox family had two daughters: Catherine, who graduated from old Oakton High School, and Wilma, who graduated from old Fairfax High School. The Fox family owned a large tract of land, and operated a dairy farm. Mr. Maurice Fox was also on the Fairfax County Board of Supervisors for a number of years, as well as active in all the community affairs. Along Hunt Road, about one-half mile north, was the dairy farm of Walter Fox and his wife. Mr. Walter Fox was a brother of Maurice Fox. This was also a large tract of land. The Walter Fox family had one son, Carrliss Fox, who worked for Fairfax County. Both Fox farms are now covered with large houses in a beautifully designed subdivision.

Another family I am familiar with is the George Loveless family. Mr. Loveless was in the wood business. He cut and hauled wood the year around, and sold same in small lots or truckloads in Fairfax County and Arlington County. Another member of the Vale community, George Hunt, was in the huckster business, and sold his produce house to house in the Fairfax and Arlington areas.

Mr. Jack Clark was a farmer and was in the charcoal business. Charcoal was used in the heating of soldering irons in the tin-roofing business. The process for making charcoal was to use pinewood 4 to 8 feet long and 2 to 5 inches in diameter. It was fired in a kiln, which took from 24 to 36 hours. The sticks of wood would be stacked on their ends in a circle in a pit about 2 feet deep and possibly 20 to 30 feet in diameter. They were covered with 4 to 6 inches of packed dirt, with small openings in the top and bottom of the kiln. The wood in the pile would be set on fire and allowed to burn until all the wood in the kiln had been burned, due to the lack of oxygen during the burning process. What was left was dark, porous, and highly flammable, with an intense rate of heat when burned in a portable soldering iron heating device. Mr. Clark sold this product in Georgetown, DC, for $1.00 per gunnysack. The firing process, as stated, took a period of time, and had to be guarded to prevent a dirt cave-in on the pile, and if a cave-in occurred, to cover same before the pile was completely consumed. Mr. Clark's son, Hammon, who was a friend, drew this duty, and he also sold the products to tinners in Georgetown, DC. Depending on the kiln size, a kiln could produce from 50 to 100 hundred bags of tinners' charcoal. This operation was a hot and dirty one, and money obtained this way was well-earned, even if during the Great Depression.

Admiral D.V. Gallery also had his home in the Vale area after World War II. The admiral won fame for himself and his crew in the capture of a German submarine and crew off the coast of Africa in the Atlantic Ocean. This capture aided the U.S. Navy in breaking the back of the German submarine fleet in World War II.

13.6 Vale Elementary School, now a community hall, 1978.
Photograph by Vincent Sutphin

13.7 Vale Elementary School, looking southwest towards the school, 1978.
Photograph by Vincent Sutphin

13.8 Vale Methodist Church and cemetery, 1978.
Photograph by Vincent Sutphin

CHAPTER 13   *Waples Mill Community*

The old two-room Vale School, used until the early 1930s by Fairfax County, still stands and is used as a community center. The Vale Methodist Church and graveyard are still in use today, which is unusual. My mother, during the 1890s, attended many affairs there when she was a young woman, and was well acquainted with all the people mentioned in this article.

The other house I wish to talk about is Squirrel Hill, located at 3416 Lyrac Street, off Vale Road. This house, as I knew it, was known as "The Kitchen Home." I have been told numerous times the property was occupied by the Waple family when they first moved into this area from Pennsylvania, before the Civil War. I visit this house in today's setting and it makes me proud and happy to thank God for the people who have restored same, and maintained this property so our young people can have some idea of our past, and how things used to be.

13.9 Squirrel Hill, former home of the Waple family, now located at 3416 Lyrac Street in the Vale area. During my time, this house was occupied by members of the Kitchen family.
Courtesy of Lee Hubbard

Nothing Remains the Same

13.10 Squirrel Hill outbuildings.
Courtesy Lee Hubbard

We return now to the Waples Mill section, as my memory does not permit me to continue to discuss additional locations in the Vale area, and the friends with whom I grew up are unavailable to help me.

Chapter 14

Waples Mill Area

Property 227

The George and Nancy Clark Waple family owned several pieces of property at the Waples Mill Road and Fox Mill Road intersection for a total of over 40 acres. No attempt by me to discuss this property's size will be made. The family members were Ralph, Rufus, Raymond, George Henry, Hazel, Florence, Lucy, and Frances. Mr. and Mrs. Waple, as all members of the family, were friendly and good neighbors. That is why today this area bears their name and not the pre-Civil War name of Fox Mill. The Fox Mill was burned by Union troops at the beginning of the Civil War. The first piece of Waple property to be discussed contained the mill location, the millrace, one of the Waple homes, the fishpond, Difficult Run, and the bridge carrying the road over the run. The property was bounded on the northwest by Waples Mill Road and

14.1 Property 227, Waples Mill millrace north of Fairfax Farm, 1981.
Courtesy of Lee Hubbard

14.2 Property 227, Waples Mill millrace.

CHAPTER 14   *Waples Mill Area*

14.3   Property 227, Waples Mill millrace.

14.4   Property 227, Waples Mill millrace.

14.5　Property 227, Waples Mill millrace.

14.6　Property 227, Difficult Run in Waples Mill site.

a section of the millrace, on the east by Difficult Run, on the south by the Neff property, now the Fairfax Farms subdivision, and on the west by the millrace, as the mill dam was located on the Neff property. The dam site was visited by me during the 1980s. Following this visit, I contacted Mr. Mike Johnson, an archaeologist with the Fairfax County Park Authority. He and I walked the site. In 1988 Mr. Johnson prepared an excellent report (on file in Fairfax County), in which he covers the dam in detail.

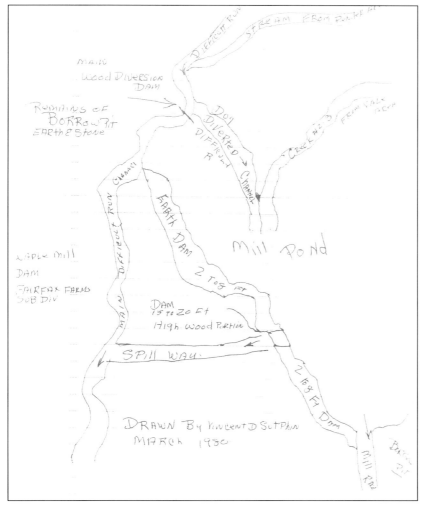

14.7 Property 227, Waples Mill dam site drawing.

I have included my hand-drawn map of the dam here. A recent visit by me again to the Fairfax Farms subdivision found expensive housing construction underway in this area. Home contractors have installed paved walkways in the general area of the old Waples Mill dam site. This makes me more than proud of the visit I made in the 1980s.

14.8 Property 227, the beginning of the pond end of the Waples Mill millrace, 1981. Left to right: Steve St. Clair, D. Sheads, V. Sutphin.
Courtesy of Lee Hubbard

14.9 Property 227, "The way we were" feature with photograph of the Waple family's grist mill.

The way we were

This undated photograph shows the Waple family's grist mill, west of Fairfax City. It is long gone, as are Keene Mill in Burke, Hunter Mill in Vienna, Arlington Mill in Arlington, Cloude's Mill in Alexandria, Nelson Mill in McLean, and Patterson Mill at the Chain Bridge. Photo courtesy of the Fairfax County Public Library Photographic Archive.

CHAPTER 14 *Waples Mill Area*

14.10 Property 228, rear view of home today occupying the old Waples Mill site.

Property 228

Property on the north side of Waples Mill Road contained a country store at the northwest corner of the intersection of Waples Mill Road and Fox Mill Road. This store was run by Mr. Waple. During the late 1930s, Mr. Waple had the store moved across the road to the old mill site and converted into a dwelling.

14.11 Property 228A, the Waple house.

Nothing Remains the Same

Property 228A

Also on the north side of the property, approximately 300 feet west of the store, was the Waple home. This was a large, two-story, frame house, painted, and well-kept. The number of acres in the Waple property is approximately 40. Mr. Waple farmed the land, ran the store and mill, and also ran a huckster business. Along with Mr. Waple's other activities, he found time to have a large fishpond constructed on the property on the south side of Waples Mill Road. This pond must have contained approximately 1 acre of property, was spring fed, and provided an excellent ice-skating rink in the winter.

Property 229

Continuing west on Waples Mill Road past the Waple home, during the early 1940s, Mr. Clark Jones and his wife, Hazel Waple Jones, built a Cape Cod, brick home on a small lot. Mr. Jones was employed as a market manager in Washington, DC. The Jones family had two children, Shirley and Edward.

Property 230

The next property consisted of several acres, and was owned by Mr. James Alexander Long, who was in the huckster business. He drove a Model T Ford car during the 1930s. Mr. Long must have been near 80 years old. I met Mr. Long's son, Lawrence, and Doris Tillett Long, Lawrence's wife, at Ocala, Florida, on a trip with William Tillett to that state during the 1980s. Mr. Lawrence Long had graduated from old Oakton High School in 1925, and had married William Tillet's aunt during the 1930s. The Long property was located at the large left-angle turn in Waples Mill Road on the northwest side, and contained a two-story, frame house and several outbuildings. Wade Bennett later acquired this property. The property is now covered with a subdivision and a number of nice homes.

Property 231

The next property on the west side of Waples Mill Road contained a two-story, frame house, acreage unknown. I have been told that this property was occupied by Garner and Ray Haines before World War I. The Coyner family also lived on this property. This occupation terminated when Mr. Coyner started to work for the Willard family in the Town of Fairfax. Known members of the Coyner family are Nellie, Evelyn, and Lewis. This property was later acquired by Major Kinsley. It is now time for me to direct my attention to the east side of Waples Mill Road, and return to my point of beginning.

Waples Mill Road and the Southeast Side

14.12 Property 232, the first home of Mr. and Mrs. George H. Waple at 11701 Waples Mill Road. During the late 1930s, this property was occupied by a retired Army sergeant, Sergeant Smith, and his wife. Sgt. Smith cared for General Pershing's horses on this property.
Photograph by Hugh Waple

Property 232

This first property is located at 11701 Waples Mill Road. During the late 1930s, this property was acquired by ex-army Cavalry Sergeant Smith and his wife. The sergeant was a veteran of World War I and a former orderly for General J.J. Pershing. Sergeant Smith had retired from the Army and was to care for General Pershing's two horses. This was before the Remount Station was completed at Front Royal, Virginia. Sergeant Smith and his wife were a wonderful couple. Mrs. Smith was French. If this couple had children, they were unknown by me.

Property 233

We now reverse the direction of our travel on the east side of Waples Mill Road. This was a good size farm owned by Mr. and Mrs. Meadow, who were an elderly couple during the 1930s. This couple sold the farm and cattle and, I am told, returned to Minnesota or some other Midwestern state. During the late 1930s, this farm was acquired by Mr. Rufus Waple. Mr. Waple and Mr. Martin Everhart set up a horse-training farm with racehorses at this location. Mr. Martin and his wife, Lillian Everhart, lived in the farmhouse. Mr. Everhart was well versed in the training of racehorses, and handled this end of the operation. After Mr. Waple closed this operation down, Mr. Martin (Bus) Everhart and Mrs. Everhart returned to Loudoun County, where Mr. Everhart continued with the horse-training occupation. The Everhart family had one child, Betty Lou, who worked for Fairfax County, and a son. Raymond Waple and his wife acquired several acres next to the farm his brother farmed, where he built several houses and sold them.

Property 234

Fairfax County purchased sufficient land in this area to build an elementary school and I am pleased that it was named Waples Mill Elementary.

Property 235

Due to a large curve in Waples Mill Road at this point, our direction will continue east. The property from the curve to the Waple Mill race was owned by Thomas Legg and his wife, Lelia Waple Legg, who were the proud parents of Percy, Malcolm, Marshall, Earl, and David. The size of this property is unknown. Mr. Legg farmed, and was also in the huckster business. The Legg family lived in a large, two-story house, painted, and well-kept. The Legg boys attended school in local elementary schools and old Oakton High School. Percy graduated from old Oakton High School; Earl and David from old Fairfax High School; Marshall from a New England school; and where Malcolm attended high school other than Oakton is unknown. During the late 1930s, Mr. and Mrs. Legg sold a portion of this property with the house to retired Master Sergeant Hugh Mottern and his French wife, Juliette. The Mottern family had four children: two daughters, Betty E. and Huguette, and two sons, Bruce and George L.

14.13 Property 236, the Thomas and Lelia Waple Legg house. The Leggs built this house in the late 1930s on the foundation of the John Henry Waple dwelling. The house is approximately 800 feet southeast of the intersection of Waples Mill Road and Fox Mill Road, a small distance west of the old Waples Mill millrace remains.

14.14 Property 236, John Henry Waple's original 1861 dwelling.

14.15 Property 236, John Henry Waple, George Henry Waple, Hezekiah S. Waple.

CHAPTER 14 *Waples Mill Area*

14.16 Property 236, Home of John Henry Waple at Waples Mill with family members on porch, circa 1896.

14.17 "The way we were" feature with photograph of men of the Waple family after a rabbit hunt.

Nothing Remains the Same **181**

Property 236

After the Leggs sold this property, they moved to what I call the old John Henry Waple house location, which faced the Waples Mill head race and was back about 200 feet on the south side of Waples Mill Road. Mr. and Mrs. Legg had a similar home built on the old John Waple home foundation, which had burned during the past.

This concludes this section of Waples Mill. We go now to the Oakton Road section.

Chapter 15

Oakton Road

15.1 Property 206, the athletic field of Flint Hill School located on Oakton Road.
Photograph by Lee Hubbard, April 2009

Property 206

Starting near this intersection of Oakton and Jermantown roads, on the north side, the first property was owned and occupied by the Allen Weaver family. Mr. and Mrs. Weaver were the parents of one son, Bernard, with whom I was well acquainted. He attended Oakton elementary and high schools, and was a veteran of World War II. Before the war, he worked as an auto mechanic, and returned to that vocation after World War II. During the period I am discussing here, Mr. Allen Weaver worked at various jobs wherever he could find work. During Mr. Weaver's younger years he made quite a name for himself as a baseball player. Many are the stories heard around Fairfax when I was a small and growing boy about the pitching ability of Mr. Weaver. Mr. Weaver received a major league tryout with the old Washington Senators when Clark Griffith was the owner. The only remark I choose to quote is, "Mr. Weaver, you have a million dollar arm." Mr. Weaver was never signed as a pitcher by the Washington team. During the 1930s Mr. Weaver, in his 40s, could still pitch for several innings. As a young boy, I saw him do so on several occasions at the old Fairfax Ball Diamond, now the property of Paul VI Catholic High School.

CHAPTER 15 *Oakton Road*

15.2 Property 207, located at 10911 Oakton Road.
Photograph by Lee Hubbard, April 2009

Property 207

The next property was owned by the Graw family. This family consisted of three children who attended Oakton elementary and high schools the same time I did. They were William, Llewellyn, and Iola. I am unable to come up with their parents' names or the size of this property. The house was two stories and of frame construction. It sat back off Oakton Road more than 100 feet.

15.3 Property 208, the location of the Roy Williams house at the present corner of Oakton Road and V Lane (formerly Marseilles Road) on the north side of Oakton Road.
Photograph by Lee Hubbard, April 2009

Property 208

The first property at the intersection of old Marseilles Lane (now V Lane) and Oakton Road was a small piece of property containing not more than an acre of ground and a small, one-room building owned by Roy Williams, who lived alone and was not married. Roy had been a World War I veteran, a member of the Civilian Conservation Corps (CCC), and, I believe, a veteran of World War II. During the period I worked for my brother Aubrey, 1938-1939, I became well acquainted with Roy. On several occasions he went to Washington with me to pick up supplies and, as I was of draft age, he was very informative to me about his experiences during World War I and with the CCC. Roy Williams was never married. He was what was then known as a loner, and had very little to say. He trusted me because I made an effort to be friendly with him, and would do him a favor when he needed one.

Property 210

The next house was small, and only occupied in the summer months by a lady whose only companions were a large collection of cats. This was in 1933. I cannot recall the lady's name or what happened to her and her companions or the property. I have never checked the records in the county. This property was located between 3361 and 3358 what is now known as "V" Lane. The lady's last name is thought to be Llewellyn.

Property 211

Only two houses occupied the northwest side of this lane. One was owned by Ed Whalen and wife. Mr. Whalen was employed by the Virginia Department of Highways as a monthly employee. He purchased his supplies at my Uncle Henry Downs' store at Jermantown and paid his bill when he received his check from the state at the end of the month.

Property 212

The other house on this side of the lane was occupied by Harvey Crowell and his wife. Mr. Crowell was a Spanish American War veteran, and received a small pension for this service. He was missing a finger on one hand. Whether this was a war wound, I never asked. He ran an account at my uncle's store and paid his bill when he received his pension check. This was a very interesting man, but I could get very little war experiences from him.

Property 209

We are on the south side of Oakton Road back from it several hundred feet. The size of this property is unknown. It was occupied by David Alexander and family. Mrs. Alexander was a daughter of Thomas Lee. Mr. and Mrs. Alexander had several children, and I am unable to give you their names at this late date.

15.4 Property 213 is now the Fellowship Baptist Church.
Photograph by Lee Hubbard, April 2009

Property 213

The next house was owned by Mr. and Mrs. Samuel Rhodes. This was a small, frame, story-and-a-half house set back some 150 to 200 feet on a small hill from Oakton Road. Mrs. Rhodes was a Waple before her marriage to Mr. Rhodes. She was blind, but could tell the difference in paper bills by their feel, and had a remarkable memory. I enjoyed delivering goods from my uncle's store and receiving cash payments from Mrs. Rhodes for same. This property is now occupied by Fellowship Baptist Church.

15.5 Property 213A, now is the Crossings of Oakton across from the Fellowship Baptist Church.
Photograph by Lee Hubbard, April 2009

Property 213A

Located on the south side of Oakton Road, across from the Fellowship Baptist Church, was property owned by the Armentrout family. This property contained from 10 to 15 acres and is now covered with large houses, and is known as the Crossing of Oakton.

Property 214

The final house on Oakton Road, before its intersection with Waples Mill Road, was owned by a former military man by the name of Wright. Mr. and Mrs. Wright purchased this property during the 1930s and built their home. They lived here for a number of years and sold it to Mr. and Mrs. Tommie Arborgast. During the 1940s, the Arborgasts' son, Hoop, and his wife built on this property on the hill next to the Armentrout property. This home had a wonderful view of the Chinn farm, Difficult Run, and valleys of the Waples Mill area.

About the Author

Photograph by Scotty W. Boatright

I have been asked to write something about myself. This, I will attempt to do. I was born November 17, 1917, at 4235 Chain Bridge Road in what is now the City of Fairfax, Virginia. My parents were Ernest J. Sutphin and Jobie T. Sutphin. My father was born in the community of New Baltimore, located on Route 211 east of Warrenton, Virginia. My mother was born in the Jermantown area near Fairfax City limits on property just west of Waples Mill Road.

After my mother and father were married in 1911 in Fairfax County near Chantilly, they purchased the property in Fairfax at 4235 Chain Bridge Road and lived there for nine years. In 1924 we moved to the Jermantown area onto a 28-acre farm which they purchased from my grandmother, Mary E. Beach Twombly. This property remained in the Beach, Twombly, and Sutphin name for over 128 years—all through the Civil War, Spanish American War, World War I and II, and the Korean War.

My parents were the father and mother of Aubrey W. Sutphin, Council M. Sutphin, Musette O. Sutphin Nevitt, Doris E. Sutphin Dunn, and myself, Vincent D. Sutphin. We had one additional brother, Ernest M. Sutphin, who died in infancy and is buried in Fairfax Cemetery.

My brother Aubrey attended Jermantown Elementary School, as well as Fairfax Elementary School. Council, Musette, Doris, and I attended Fairfax Elementary School. Aubrey and Council graduated from the old Oakton High School in 1929. My sister, Musette, and I attended the old Oakton High School for 2½ years before it closed. We were required to furnish our own transportation, as were all students who attended high school in Fairfax County at that time. My sisters, Musette and Doris, graduated from Fairfax High School after normal terms. I had to be different; I received my diploma in 1961 after attending night school.

My working experience started at an early age, around nine, under the supervision of my father, mother, and brother, Council. On a working farm, you start early. The farm animals must be fed and given water. Wood must be carried to the house from the wood shed. Corn has to be shelled for the chickens. Eggs have to be gathered from the nests in the chicken house, and vegetables worked and picked in the garden. You were also expected to do what you could toward raising and harvesting the field crops. We learned to replant corn and thin it. We even helped in the neighbors' fields. On Saturdays, at around the age of fourteen, I started to help Russell Haines. Mr. Haines was a local huckster who sold produce at the Washington Farmers Market. This produce consisted of dressed chickens and other items, including butter and eggs; fresh and country hams; country sausage and pork products.

As I grew older, I was expected to advance in my work knowledge and take on more responsibility. During my freshman year at Oakton High School, I started taking agriculture, general science, English, and mathematics. Generally, I found these subjects to my liking and no trouble. This was during the Great Depression. The $1.50 per day earned by me for helping Russell Haines on the market on Saturdays from 4:00 AM to 8:00 PM came to good use for school expenses, clothing, and other items.

At the end of school in June, my uncle, Henry Downs, had a stroke which disabled him for several months. I went to live with my grandmother, aunt, and Uncle Henry to look after the cows and aid in the general store, which was owned by the Downs. I was no longer able to help Russell Haines in the huckster business on Saturday. These new duties with my uncle required driving a small truck and the delivery of feed and groceries. My mother provided the necessary signature for securing a Virginia driver's permit. I continued to help my uncle and brother, Aubrey, for about six months and returned home to take up aiding my father on the farm. During the spring of 1935, Fruit Growers Express Company (a railroad refrigeration company in the Alexandria area) began hiring men. My brother, Council, who was working for Russell Haines in the huckster business, applied for a job and was accepted. He continued to work for this company until he retired.

Russell Haines asked me if I would help him on Saturdays, selling produce at the Farmers Market in Washington. Of course, I said yes. This continued until spring 1936 when I was hospitalized for a hernia operation, primarily because of too much basketball in high school. This, and lack of proper attention to school work, caused my failure to graduate with my class on June 5, 1936.

After recuperating from the operation in May 1936, I started a part-time job with the Sanitary Grocery Company in Fairfax. This job expanded to full-time in September in Alexandria, and later in McLean and Arlington at different stores until spring 1938 when I quit and accepted a job with my brother, Aubrey, in the general store he had purchased in 1935 from our Uncle Henry at Jermantown. This arrangement continued only until summer 1939 due to financial conditions. My brother accepted bankruptcy. I went back to work for Safeway grocery stores in Fairfax and Arlington counties, and in the City of Alexandria. This arrangement continued until spring 1941, when I accepted a position of meter reader in the newly-opened Fairfax office of Virginia Public Service Company (now VEPCO).

Now this was an entirely new type of work and for a public utility company paying me $23.00 per 40-hour week, lunch expenses of 50 cents per day, and use of a vehicle on the job—as opposed to a 54-hour work week for $25.00 and having to drive my car to whatever store Safeway had wanted me to work that day. My work with this company progressed. I continued to advance until September 25, 1942, when I was accepted for service in the United States Army at Camp Lee, Virginia. After an examination in Richmond, I experienced a rushed trip to Petersburg by train to Camp Lee and no supper after arrival at the army base, but a mattress and a cot to sleep on.

Army routine started at 6:00 AM. My duties included keeping the coal fires burning in several barracks for water heaters for showers. On Monday morning I was relieved of these duties and was issued uniforms, given shots, received instructions, and given tests. I was then ready to be shipped out to Fort Knox, Kentucky, by Wednesday.

On the upcoming Monday, I started basic training for the Armed Forces of the United States. This basic training went on for thirteen weeks. When this period was over, I was assigned to my permanent outfit, the 781 Tank Battalion, which I continued to be a part of for the three-year period I was in the army during World War II. I was a tank gunner and crew member the last fifteen months. Before that time, I had worked the Battalion Post Office and Message Center at Fort Knox for this same outfit.

My outfit shipped to Europe and landed at Marseille in southern France in October, 1944, where I joined the 7th American Army and went into action against the German army with 100 American Infantry Division in the old German-manned Maginot Line Fortresses at Bitche, France, on or about December 15, 1944. My outfit fought with as many as five different American infantry divisions and had continuous contact with the German army for over 180 days. Near the end of World War II, in May 1945, we returned to the United States for thirty days rest and resupply, readying for redeployment to the Pacific for the invasion of Japan scheduled for November 1945. This didn't happen because President Truman ordered the atomic bomb dropped, ending this conflict while I was on leave in August.

After returning to my outfit at Camp Campbell, Kentucky, in late August, it was only a short time before I was discharged and resumed my employment with a new utility company in Fairfax: the Virginia Electric and Power Company (VEPCO). To summarize my army career, I had fun away from home for years, had earned three battle stars, had been overseas for only nine months, had not been injured, and had been married for a period of over a year and was the father of a beautiful young daughter by the name of Linda Ann. I was ready to resume my career when I arrived home on a Thursday and started work on the following Monday.

I found out I was to be called a "line truck driver," as two older men now occupied my former position of meter reader. I soon found out I did not have one duty, but was being used for a number of different jobs—more or less like a utility man. I loved this type of assignment. Continuing on this assignment for about three months, I was asked if I would accept a position in the engineering department with a base monthly salary and 40-hour work week. I asked how much did this position pay. I was told $140.00 plus overtime over 40 hours per week. I liked the opportunity and thanked them for the consideration. So, the first of the month of April 1946, I started my new duties. Over the next twenty years, I advanced two levels and performed a number of different duties related to engineering, administration, supervision, trouble-shooting, and public relations. The last thirteen years I was employed by the company was with system construction, which had to do with the supervision of contract bid jobs by other companies. I then returned to the Alexandria office for one year before retiring in June 1983 after 42 years with VEPCO.

After retiring, I had to have something to do so I talked Bill Tillett, a public auctioneer, into letting me hang around his auction barn at no pay. He wanted to pay me, but I wanted my freedom to be able to travel and have no obligations. I needed to feel wanted and that there was still some use for me. I continued to do this until about 2006, when any type of work was too much. I quit and finished up my book, *Nothing Remains the Same*. I am satisfied now to do nothing except talk, read, and shake hands.

In closing I think we all look back to what we have accomplished. I saw a whole lot, having lived during the period of 1917 to the present day. One of the biggest things I accomplished was collecting over $3300 from battalion members of my military outfit—the 781 Tank Battalion—for a monument. I saw that it was erected on the grounds of Patton Museum at Fort Knox, Kentucky, in memory of the 37 members of the outfit who gave their lives so the others of the outfit could live free in this beautiful country of ours. Thinking back, this is what I consider the greatest accomplishment in my life.

Acknowledgments

After so many years, this project would have been impossible without the additional help from my many friends. These friends to whom I am indebted are as follows: Lee Hubbard, Hugh Waple, Fred Kielsgard, Alice Allder, John F. Swart, Agnes Moore, Shirley Sherwood Van Fleet, Becky Sherwood Keys, Professor Cullen Sherwood, Bill Tillett, Claudette Crouch Ward, Gwen Beck, American Legion Post #177, Fairfax VFW Post #8469, Bill Sisson, Bill Anderson, Bob Waple, Ed Beck, Joan Hubbard, and Margaret Peck.

Name Index

A

Alexander, David, 187
Allbright, Maggie Ballard, 115–16
Allder, Agnes, 115
Allder, Alice, 196
Allder, Edna May Swart, 145
Allder, F.M., 17, 18
Allder, Flavius B., 115
Allder, Flavius M., 115
Allder, Frankie Fox, 115
Allder, Madeline, 115
Allder, Marshall, 115, 128–29
Allder, Mary Robertson, 128
Allder, Mr., 106
Allder, Myrtle Swart, 145
Allder, Paul F., 145
Allder, Paul, 115
Allder, Roy, 115, 145
Allison, Robert, 16
Ambler, Mary O., 73
Anderson family, 46
Anderson, Bill, 196
Anderson, Gary, 37
Anderson, George D., 37
Anderson, George, 36
Anderson, Jim, 37
Anderson, Lucille, 36
Arborgast, Austin, 47, 49
Arborgast, Austin, 51
Arborgast, Hoop, 189
Arborgast, Tommie, 189
Arborgast, Vina, 51
Armand family, 152
Armentrout family, 188
Ashton, Becky, 18
Ashton, Fred, 18
Aston, John W., 46
Aylor, B., 86

B

Bacon, Nathaniel, 68
Ball, Bessie, 25
Ballard family, 115–16
Barrett, Kate Waller, 73–74
Beach, Ann Marie Markell, 57
Beach, Forrest, 28
Beach, George W., 57, 64
Beach, George, 18, 22, 28, 73–74
Beach, Martha W., 28
Beach, Martha Worster, 22, 57
Beach, Martha, 28
Beach, Mary E., 57
Beach, Sampson, 57
Beach, Samuel, 64
Beck, Ed, 196
Beck, Gwen, 133, 196
Bennett, Wade, 176
Berkey, Macell, 51
Berkey, O.L., 51
Berkley, Lizzie, 141
Berkley, William, 141
Bernaugh, Nancy, 13, 18
Birch, Alvin, 105–6
Birch, Mary James, 105–6
Birch, Melvin, 105–6
Birch, Phyllis, 105
Birch, Ralph, 105
Birch, Ray, 105–10
Blevins, Frank, 79
Blevins, Tom, 74
Booker, David, 54

Bowers, Blanch Haines, 42
Bowers, Lloyd, 42
Bowman, Christine, 98
Bowman, Louise, 97
Bradford, Mayonie Moore, 83
Breeden family, 164
Brooks, Annie Poland, 37
Brooks, Paul, 37
Brown, Margaret Dawson, 86
Brown, Sara Eileen Dawson, 86
Bryce family, 94
Bryce, Fannie Stewart, 123
Bryce, Lyman H., 123
Buckley, Alexander, 139
Buckley, John, 151
Buckley, Mary Ann, 139
Burke, Gus, 144–46
Burleigh, Dewey H., Jr., 162
Byrne, Betty Jane, 114
Byrne, Dorothy, 114
Byrne, Fielding Littleton, 102
Byrne, George, 106, 114
Byrne, Minnie Lambert, 102
Byrns, Laura, 46, 51

C

Campbell, Isabell Sherwood, 89
Carpender, Charles, 81
Carpender, Ester Robey, 81
Carter, George, 85
Carter, Harriet Lamb, 85
Chambers, Dick, 19
Chambers, Mr., 70
Chinn, Charlie, 163
Chinn, Dora, 163

Chinn, John, 157, 162–64
Chinn, Minnie, 157, 163
Chinn, Sam, 163
Chinn, Sara, 162
Chinn, Tom, 163
Christeller, Oscar, 13
Clark, Hammon, 165
Clark, Jack, 165
Clark, Sara Summers, 160
Clarke, J., 19, 38
Clarke, Margaret, 19
Coe, William Gwynn, 17
Colbert, Clarence, 18, 70–71
Colbert, Jake, 18, 70–71
Colley, Charles H., 108-9
Collins, O.J., 157
Cook family, 8, 70
Cook, Anna, 25
Cornell, R.L., 51
Coyner, Evelyn, 177
Coyner, Lewis, 177
Coyner, Nellie, 177
Craig, Clarice Haines, 42, 64
Craig, Harry, 105
Craig, Isaac, 42, 64
Cronk, Ann, 85
Cronk, Greenberry, 86
Cronk, Sara J. Thompson, 86
Croson, Bernice, 114
Croson, Joe, 114, 120
Croson, Louellen, 120
Croson, Louise, 120
Croson, Ralph, 120
Croson, Roy, 103, 114
Croson, Serena, 114
Croson, Welby, 120–21
Cross, Barbara, 118
Cross, Madeline, 96, 118
Cross, Nell, 118
Cross, Wallace, 96, 118
Cross, William, 118
Crouch, Abbie Buckley, 139
Crouch, Carrie Thompson, 146
Crouch, John Leo, 146
Crouch, John, 146
Crouch, Lorraine, 146
Crouch, Myrtle, 146
Crouch, Norman, 139
Crouch, Wilton Lee, 146
Crowell, Harvey, 186–87

D

Dalaney, J.H., 17
Dawson, Ann V., 86
Dawson, Edwin, 86
Dawson, Elsie R., 86
Dawson, Jane, 86
Dawson, Margaret, 86
Dawson, Sara Eileen, 86
Dawson, Tom, 86
Dennis, Ethel Mickelson, 81
Denny, Annie, 67
Denny, Collins, 17
Denny, David, 67
Denny, E.D., 67
Denny, Earnest, 67
Denny, Edith, 67, 99
Denny, Ellen, 67
Denny, Eugene, 67
Denny, George, 67
Denny, John, 67
Denny, Judy, 67
Denny, William, 67
Dindlebeck, Clayton, 8
Dindlebeck, Grace, 8
Dindlebeck, Louis, 8
Dindlebeck, Mamie, 8
Dindlebeck, Mary V. Sisson, 8
Dindlebeck, Robert, 8
Dirbershier family, 14
Dodson, Betty Jane Byrne, 114
Dodson, Clark, 114
Downs, Gladys Sherwood, 89
Downs, Henry, 38, 60, 192
Downs, Nellie Twombly, 25, 46, 49
Downs, Richard H., 25, 47
Downs, Richard Henry, 46
Driscoll, Pat, 23
Dunbar family, 128
Dunn, Doris E. Sutphin, 58, 191–92

E

Edmond, Virginia, 42
Eliott, Miss, 73
Ellis family, 74
Erskine, Mr., 36
Everhart, Betty Lou, 178
Everhart, Lillian Hutchinson, 94
Everhart, Lillian, 178
Everhart, Martin, 178

F

Fendley, Mary Agnes Moore, 83
Ferguson, Hazel, 141
Ferguson, Judge, 141
Fleming, Aline A., 114
Fleming, Benjamin C., 114
Fletcher, Elizabeth C., 94
Fox, Carrliss, 164
Fox, Catherine, 164
Fox, Frankie, 115
Fox, Mamie, 105
Fox, Maurice, 164–65
Fox, Nora, 105
Fox, Otis, 105
Fox, Sylvester, 105
Fox, Walter, 164–65
Fox, Wilma, 164

G

Gallery, D.V., 165
Gheen, Ernest, 97
Gheen, Irene, 97
Gheen, Jack, 97
Gheen, Louise Bowman, 97
Gheen, Maurice, 97
Gibson, Fannie, 123
Gooding, Bessie, 115
Gooding, Lula May, 145
Gooding, Ray, 115
Goodnow, David, 53, 56
Goodnow, Nellie Robey, 56
Graham, Harry, 23
Graw, Iola, 185
Graw, Llewellyn, 185

Name Index

Graw, William, 185
Green, L.H., 73, 96
Greenstreet family, 158
Griffith, Clark, 184

H

Hailman family, 12
Haines family, 17
Haines, Alice, 145–46
Haines, Blanch, 42
Haines, Clarence, 42
Haines, Clarice, 42
Haines, Ethel, 33, 42, 50
Haines, Garner, 177
Haines, Lena F. Powell, 42
Haines, Leo, 16, 42, 135–36
Haines, Ray, 177
Haines, Robert D., 41–42
Haines, Robert Ray, 42
Haines, Rose J., 144
Haines, Rose May Jerman, 41, 86
Haines, Russell, 41–42, 157, 192–93
Haines, Susan Ross, 42
Haines, Virginia Edmond, 42
Haines, Virginia, 42
Haines, William Garner, 42
Haley, James, 80
Hall, George, 16
Hall, Ida M., 16
Hall, Jenny, 157–58
Hall, Lou, 157–58
Hall, Oliver F., 162
Harrison, Florence, 9, 12
Harrison, Tom, 144
Harrison, William, 9, 12
Hawes, Archie, 37
Higgdon, Mr., 36
Horton, Buck, 18
Howard, Henrietta V., 123
Hubbard, Joan, 196
Hubbard, Lee, 196
Huddleston, F.W., 36
Hunt, George, 165
Hutchinson, Aubrey W., 94
Hutchinson, Elizabeth C. Fletcher, 94
Hutchinson, Ira, 94
Hutchinson, Lillian, 94
Hutchinson, Randolph, 94

I

Isdell, Dottie, 133
Isdell, Mary, 133

J

Jackson, John E., 156
Jackson, John, 18
Jackson, Lucy, 18, 156
Jerman, Elmer, 36, 74
Jerman, Hezekiah, 23
Jerman, John, 73, 75
Jerman, M.G., 17
Jerman, Milton, 86
Jerman, Rose May, 41
Jerman, Smith, 8, 23
Johnson, Harold, 162
Johnson, Mike, 173
Jones, Clark, 176
Jones, Edward, 176
Jones, Hazel Waple, 176
Jones, Shirley, 176

K

Keen family, 74
Keys, Becky Sherwood, 196
Kidwell, Archie, 98
Kidwell, Berkeley, 75
Kidwell, Berkley, 98
Kidwell, Christine Bowman, 98
Kidwell, Durley Sutphin, 98
Kidwell, Elsie, 98
Kidwell, Ethel Makley, 98
Kidwell, Florence, 113
Kidwell, Leish, 98
Kidwell, Maude R., 75
Kidwell, Maude Roberson, 98
Kidwell, Rose E. Lightfoot, 98
Kidwell, Tommie, 97–98
Kidwell, Vernon, 103, 113
Kidwell, Wesley, 98
Kielsgard, Bramwell, 88
Kielsgard, Fred, 88, 196
Kielsgard, Miller S., 103
Kielsgard, Miller, 79, 128
King, James, 37
Kinsley, Major, 177
Kline, Annie J., 131–32
Kline, Charlie, 131–32

L

Lambert, Minnie, 102
Lee, Annie Waple, 159
Lee, Bernice, 159
Lee, Blanche, 159
Lee, Effie M., 159
Lee, Fay, 159
Lee, George B., 159
Lee, George E., 159
Lee, Helen B., 159
Lee, Ida B. Wells, 159
Lee, Lelia, 159
Lee, Marion N., 159
Lee, Martha Jane Monroe, 159
Lee, Norman, 159
Lee, Ruben M., 159
Lee, Thomas F., 159
Lee, Thomas, 159, 187
Lee, Tom, 23
Lee, Walton B., 159
Lee, William, 159
Legg, David, 178
Legg, Earl, 178
Legg, Lelia Waple, 178–79, 182
Legg, Malcolm, 178–79
Legg, Marshall, 178–79
Legg, Percy, 178
Legg, Thomas, 178–79, 182
Lehman, Walter, 144
Lightfoot, Rose E., 98
Lightfoot, Sam, 134–35
Long, Doris Tillett, 176
Long, James Alexander, 176
Long, Lawrence, 176
Loveless, George, 165
Lucas, Cindy, 18–19
Lunceford, Shirley, 70

M

Makley, Ethel, 98
Manuel family, 130
Markell, Ann Marie, 57
Martin family, 114
Martin, Nellie T., 159
Matthews, Phillip, 68
Matthews, Sadie, 68
Matthews, Salome N., 68
McCarthy, Joe, 102
McCarthy, William M., 102
McFarland, Douglas, 78
Meadow family, 178
Mickelson, Ethel, 81
Mickelson, Mr., 81
Millan family, 14, 135, 149–50
Millan, Lillian, 16, 135–36, 149–50
Millan, Mary, 135–36, 149–50
Millan, Thomas, 94
Miller, Edward X., 33
Miller, Pauline Sherwood, 33
Millicent, Ralph Leroy, 160
Mills family, 46, 128
Mills, Annie, 85
Mills, Harry, 79
Mohr family, 152
Molock, Fred, 162
Monroe, Deskin, 23, 159
Monroe, Martha Jane, 159
Moore, Agnes, 196
Moore, Alice Morris, 83
Moore, Barbara, 83
Moore, Ed, 104
Moore, Edward B., 82–83
Moore, George R., 82
Moore, James W., 104
Moore, James, 104
Moore, Jim, 13
Moore, John, 104
Moore, Julie R., 104
Moore, Kate, 104
Moore, Lillian S., 13
Moore, Mary Agnes, 83
Moore, Mattie Sutphin, 82–83
Moore, Mayonie, 83
Moore, Mike, 104
Moore, Nora, 104
Moore, Phillip H., 83
Mosby, John S., 86, 123
Mottern, Betty E., 179
Mottern, Bruce, 179
Mottern, George L., 179
Mottern, Hugh, 179
Mottern, Huguette, 179
Mottern, Juliette, 179
Mountford, Hollis R., 107-8
Mozingo family, 96
Mulholland, John, 80
Mulholland, Pete, 80
Murry, John J., 46
Myers, Glen, 144

N

Nachman, Ann V. Dawson, 86
Neff family, 67, 162
Neff, E.E., 67
Nevitte, Musette Sutphin, 58, 60, 191–92
Newman, Adrian, 144
Newman, America, 144
Newman, Benjamin, 144
Newman, Frances, 144
Newman, William, 144
Nork, Auther, 104
Nork, Louise, 104

O

O'Bannon, Cecil, 85
O'Bannon, Corbin, 81, 85
O'Bannon, Lizzy, 81, 85

P

Palmer, H.M.F., 146
Payne, Charity, 18, 78
Payne, Charley, 18
Payne, Melinda, 118
Payne, Washington, 18, 78
Peck, Margaret, 196
Pershing, J.J., 177
Poirier, Bernard W., 108
Poland, Annie, 37
Poland, Guy, 36
Poland, Helen, 36
Potterton, Gladys Sisson, 134
Powell, Lena F., 74

R

Rhodes, Samuel, 187
Rhodes, Stella Waple, 158–59, 187
Rice, Paul, 157
Richardson, Maggie, 85
Richardson, William, 85
Riley, Mr., 71
Roberson, Ann Cronk, 85
Roberson, Edith, 85
Roberson, Elsie, 85
Roberson, George, 85
Roberson, Ira, 85
Roberson, Maude, 98
Roberson, Oswald, 85
Robertson, Earnest, 129–31
Robertson, Elliott, 129
Robertson, George, 131
Robertson, John, 129
Robertson, Kathleen, 129
Robertson, Louie, 74
Robertson, Minnie Kline, 129–31
Robertson, Richard, 74
Robertson, Warren, 162
Robey, Ester, 81
Robey, Lutie, 135
Robey, Major, 135
Robey, Marion, 56
Robey, Nellie B., 55–56
Robey, Nellie, 56
Robey, Rodophus R., 55
Robey, Roxie, 56
Robey, Sam, 23
Robey, Sam, 54–56
Robey, Samuel, 56
Rollins, Addie M., 115
Rollins, Edgar T., 115
Rollins, Estelle, 115
Rollins, Lillian, 33
Rollins, Thomas, 115
Roosevelt, Eleanor, 146

Name Index

Rosemond, Charles C., Sr., 72
Rosemond, Charles, Jr., 72
Rosemond, Martha, 72
Ross, Susan, 42
Rowland, Barbara Moore, 83
Runner, Ben, 18, 70
Runner, Winfield, 70
Runner, Winfree, 18
Russell, Graham, 132
Russell, Jake, 146
Rust, John, 79

S

Schaefer family, 162
Scott family, 9
Scott, Charlie, 18, 71
Seaton, Jim, 30
Seek, Kathleen Robertson, 129–31
Seek, Marvin O., 129–30
Shaw, Alice L., 108-9
Sheads, D., 174
Sheets, G., 106
Sherwood, Albert R., 88
Sherwood, Albert, 78, 106
Sherwood, Alvin, 89
Sherwood, Cullen, 196
Sherwood, Edith Denny, 99
Sherwood, Elizabeth E., 31
Sherwood, Elizabeth, 88
Sherwood, Ethel Haines, 33, 42
Sherwood, Franklin, 89
Sherwood, George F., 88–89
Sherwood, Gladys, 89
Sherwood, Howard, 89
Sherwood, Isabell, 89
Sherwood, Joseph R., 88
Sherwood, Laura E., 88
Sherwood, Laura F., 31
Sherwood, Lewis, 89
Sherwood, Louis F., 88
Sherwood, Luther R., 42, 88
Sherwood, Luther, 33, 106
Sherwood, Margaret E., 88
Sherwood, Margaret F., 31
Sherwood, Maxwell C., 33
Sherwood, Maxwell, 99

Sherwood, Minnie Waple, 88–89
Sherwood, Pauline, 33
Sherwood, Quentin, 33
Sherwood, Ruth, 33
Sherwood, Sarah E. Kidwell, 88
Sherwood, Vernon, 89
Sherwood, Walter, 89
Sisson (Sam) family, 16, 134, 145
Sisson, Bill, 196
Sisson, Bob, 134
Sisson, Elhannon B., 134
Sisson, Nannie Hersey, 134
Sisson, Rosa, 134, 145
Sisson, Viola, 134, 145
Smith family, 112
Smith, Albert, 13
Smith, Lillie, 78
Smith, Mr., 134
Smith, Phyllis Birch, 105
Smith, Sergeant, 177
Smith, Will, 78
Snapp, Elizabeth E. Sherwood, 31
Snapp, James B., 31
Snapp, Louis M., 31
Snapp, Robert, 31
Spaulding family, 104–5
St. Clair, Steve, 174
Staats, E., 98
Staats, Elsie Kidwell, 98
Stanley, A.B., 80
Stewart, Charles Lewis, 123
Stewart, Charles, 123
Stewart, Eleanor, 123
Stewart, Fannie Gibson, 123
Stewart, Fannie, 123
Stewart, Frank, 96
Stewart, Henrietta V. Howard, 123
Stewart, Mamie Twombly, 25, 123
Stewart, Norman H., 123
Stewart, Norman, 25
Stoner, Mr., 1–2
Stowe, Alfred, 123
Stowe, E.F., 123
Stowe, Robert, 123
Stuart, Frank, 38
Sutphin, Aubrey W., 47, 58, 186, 191–93

Sutphin, Council, 42, 58, 191–93
Sutphin, Doris, 191–92. *See also* Dunn, Doris E. Sutphin,
Sutphin, Durley, 36, 79, 98
Sutphin, Ernest J., 1, 25, 57, 191
Sutphin, Ernest M., 191
Sutphin, Everett, 105
Sutphin, Jobie Twombly, 1, 25, 57, 191
Sutphin, John, 36, 80
Sutphin, Kate, 80
Sutphin, Leish, 79
Sutphin, Linda Ann, 118, 194
Sutphin, Mamie Fox, 105
Sutphin, Musette, 54, 191–92. *See also* Nevitte, Musette Sutphin
Sutphin, Ruth W., 51
Sutphin, Vincent, 54, 58, 174, 191–95
Sutphin, Winter, 105
Swart family, 14, 17, 40–41, 65
Swart, Asa, 40–41
Swart, Edna May, 145
Swart, Florence Harrison, 9, 12
Swart, Florence, 9
Swart, Gwendolyn, 9
Swart, Halley, 12
Swart, J. Frank, 40
Swart, James E., 39
Swart, John, 40–41
Swart, John F., 9, 12, 39–40, 50, 196
Swart, John H., 9, 12, 144
Swart, John Henry, 128
Swart, Lula May Gooding, 145
Swart, Maggie, 9
Swart, Myrtle, 145
Swart, Stacy, 9, 12
Swart, Wesley, 145

T

Taylor, James W., 25
Thompson, Albert, 94
Thompson, Carrie, 99, 146
Thompson, Edith, 153
Thompson, Elbert, 99
Thompson, Elsie, 99

Thompson, Ethel, 99
Thompson, Florence, 94
Thompson, Gilbert, 98
Thompson, Jim, 120
Thompson, Louis M., 99
Thompson, Louis, Jr., 99, 104
Thompson, Sara J., 86
Thompson, Willie, 99
Tillett, Bill, 195–96
Tillett, Doris, 176
Tillett, William, 176
Tilson family, 71
Tinder, Bertie, 113
Tinder, Marie, 113
Tinder, Milton, 113
Tinder, Myrtle, 113
Tinder, Rachael, 113
Tinder, Rodney, 113
Tinder, Ruby, 113
Tinder, William, 113
Twombly, Anna Cook, 25, 34
Twombly, Bessie Ball, 25, 33
Twombly, Claude, 33
Twombly, Eunice, 33
Twombly, George, 23, 25, 33
Twombly, Jobie, 23, 25
Twombly, Lillian Rollins, 33
Twombly, Louise, 33
Twombly, Mamie, 23, 25, 123
Twombly, Mary E. Beach, 1, 16, 22–25, 33, 34, 57, 191
Twombly, Nellie, 23, 25
Twombly, Stanley M., 23, 25, 34
Twombly, Stanley, 23
Twombly, Stephen P., 6, 16, 18, 22–25, 33–34, 57, 73, 159

V

Van Buskirk, Ralph, 107
Van Fleet, Shirley Sherwood, 196

W

Waley, A., 19, 38
Waple, Bob, 196
Waple, Florence, 170
Waple, Frances, 170
Waple, George Henry, 170, 176, 177, 180
Waple, George, 170
Waple, Hazel, 170, 176
Waple, Hezekiah S., 180
Waple, Hugh, 196
Waple, John Henry, 179–82
Waple, John, 182
Waple, Lelia, 179
Waple, Lucy, 170
Waple, Mamie Dindlebeck, 8
Waple, Nancy Clark, 170
Waple, Ralph, 8, 170
Waple, Raymond, 170, 178
Waple, Rufus, 170, 178
Ward, Claudette Crouch, 139, 196
Weaver, Allen, 184
Weaver, Bernard, 184
Webster, Charles, 105
Webster, Eva S., 105
Webster, Raymond, 105
Webster, Sarah, 105
Weller, Mark, 103
Wells, Arvine, 157, 163
Wells, George R., 70
Wells, Ida B., 159
Wells, Jacqueline, 157
Wells, Minnie Chinn, 157, 163–64
Wells, Mrs., 17
Welsh, Herb, 81
Whalen, Ed, 186
White, Frank, 130, 144
Williams, Roy, 185–86
Winfield, Gladys, 80, 132, 136
Woodrick, Charles, 128
Woodward family, 135
Wooster, Martha W., 57
Worster, Tapley, 22, 28, 30
Wright family, 189

Y

Young, Lehman, 71

Subject Index

A

AAL-Matic Transmission Service, 127
Amoco gas stations, 48–49, 120
amusement parks, 149
antique shops, 132
Arborgast's Henry J. Garage, 48–49
Arlington & Fairfax Electric Trolley, 159
assembly halls, 12
automobile dealerships, 8–9, 48–49
automobile repair shops, 126–27

B

banks. *See specific banks*
barber shops, 114, 119
Battle for Cedar Mountain, 109
Battle of Ox Hill, 28, 116–18
"A Beech Tree" (Birch), 106–10
Betty's Azalea Ranch, 139
black families, 18–19
Black Lantern Inn, 2, 8, 70
blacksmith shops, 97
Briarwood Manor, 153
Buckley Baptist Chapel, 136
butchering businesses, 86

C

Camp 30, Virginia Prison System, 73, 189
Cannon Ridge subdivision, 139
cemeteries
    Civil War, 74
    Fairfax, 57
    Fairfax County Poor House, 37
    Jermantown, 8, 85
    Kidwell-Robertson, 128
    Oakton United Brethren Church, 132
    private, 80, 141
    unnamed, 14
    Vale Methodist Church, 166–67
Center Point Church, 96
charcoal, manufacturing of, 165
Christ Presbyterian Church, 122–23
churches, 14, 17–18. *See also specific churches*
Civil War
    Battle of Ox Hill, 28, 116–18
    cemetery during, 74
    Confederate outposts during, 25, 42
    Fox Mill and, 170
    hospital, 23, 25
    initials on tree from time of, 107
    Mosby, and Warrenton Pike tollgate, during, 86
    10th Maine Volunteers, 109
    25th Maine Infantry, 107
    Union outposts during, 60–61
commercial development, Swarts and, 40–41
Confederate Camp Pettus Regional Hospital, 25
Croson store, 114, 119–20
The Crossings at Oakton subdivision, 188
Crystal Springs subdivision, 141

D

dairies/dairy farms, 12, 28, 36, 40, 147, 164
dams, 160–61, 173
dance halls, 135, 149–52
dentistry, 134
Difficult Run
    Fox Mill dam on, 160–61
    headwaters of, 88
    in Waples Mill site, 172
Difficult Run Bridge, 30–31, 65, 67
Difficult Run Hill, 26, 28, 30–31, 61
Dinner Bell Restaurant, 148–49
distilleries, 133–34, 145
Dominion Power Company, 8, 71, 123
Down's store, 13, 38, 46–47, 49, 192
drive-in theaters, 150
drovers' rests, 29–30, 38, 41
Dunkard church, 158–59

E

education, difficulty obtaining, 115

F

Fairfax Acres subdivision, 14
Fairfax Ball Diamond, 184
Fairfax Cemetery, 57
Fairfax Circuit, 17
Fairfax City, 40
Fairfax County Fire Station 40, 147
Fairfax County Poor House, 37

Fairfax County Sanitation and Waste, 150
Fairfax Court Center, 12, 41
Fairfax Fair Grounds, 36
Fairfax Farms subdivision, 67, 173
Fairfax Hardware Store, 70
Fairfax Lodge, 38
Fairfax Methodist Church, 17
Fairfax Ridge housing development, 51–52, 56–57, 59
Fairfax Towne Center, 117
Fair Oaks Church, 150
Fair Oaks District Police Station, 121
Fair Oaks Fire Station 21, 121
Fair Oaks Mall, 92–93
Fair Oaks Shopping Center, 33–34, 94, 112
Fairview Farms, 36–37
farms. *See also* dairies/dairy farms; huckster business
   German prisoners-of-war and, 73
Fellowship Baptist Church, 187–88
fire and rescue stations, 121, 147
fire tower, 114, 121
fire training station, 150
Flint High School, 184
Fox Mill, 160, 170
Fox Mill community, 156
Fox Mill dam, 160–61
Fox Mill millrace, 161
Franklin Bus Company, 104
Fruit Growers Express Company, 192–93
fruit stands, 98–99. *See also* Down's Store

G

The Gardens assisted living facility, 86
gas stations
   Amoco, 48–49, 120
   Shell, 9, 12
   Texaco, 84–85
   unnamed, 78
general stores, 22–23, 97, 131, 147
Georgious Company, 52, 57
German prisoner-of-war camp, 73, 76, 189
Giant food store, 9, 39–40
Glen Alden subdivision, 132
golf courses, 93–94, 112
Gooding farm, 145
grocery stores, 9, 39–40, 126, 144, 193

H

Happy Hour Dance Hall, 151–52
Hechinger Company, 40
Henry J. Garage, 48–49
High Banks Swimming Hole, 160
homeless shelters, 38
hospitals, 23, 25
huckster businesses, 22, 41–42, 165, 176, 178, 192
Hunters Lodge and Dance Hall, 135, 149–50

J

Jermantown area map, 3
Jermantown Cemetery, 8, 85
Jermantown Grade School, 88
Jermantown Hall, 16–17
Jermantown School, 16
Jerusalem Baptist Church, 57

K

Kamp Washington, 1–2, 36
Kidwell-Robertson Family Cemetery, 128
Kielsgarden subdivision, 88–89
Kline's general store, 131
Kunter Park, 37

L

Lee High Village subdivision, 128
"The Lees" house, 159
Legato area map, 4
Legato School, 135–36

Little River Turnpike
   construction of Milestone 17, 112
   milestone markers on, 36
   single arch bridge on, 30–31, 65, 67
   tollhouse for, 67
log houses
   Buckley dwelling, 137–39
   Harrison home, 12
   Moore home, 82
   Squirrel Hill, 167–68

M

Manuel Tourist Court and Restaurant, 129–30
markers, roadside, 36
Marymead Drive, 133
Merrifield Garden Center, 133–34, 145
Milestone 15, 36
Milestone 16, 61, 65
Milestone 17, 112
milestone markers, 36
Millan School House, 17
mills. *See also* sawmill businesses
   Fox Mill, 160, 170
   Waples Mill, 174
movie theaters, drive-in, 150
My Home Shop, 139

N

National Bank of Fairfax, 40
Navy community, 156
nurseries, plant, 84–85, 139
nursing homes, 38

O

Oak Hill, 56
Oakton High School, 113, 115
Oakton United Brethren Church Cemetery, 132

Subject Index

P

Palmer store. *See* Russell store
Paul VI Catholic High School, 184
Pender area map, 5
Penderbrook subdivision, 112
Pender Methodist Church, 17–18, 94–96
Pender School, 103
Pender United Methodist Church, 122–23
Pender Veterinary Clinic, 94
picnic areas, 46, 50–51
Piney Ridge Farm, 121–23
plant nurseries, 84–85, 139
poplar tree in Swart woods, 64–65
potter's fields. *See* cemeteries
poultry and egg businesses, 72, 81, 147, 159
prison camp, 73, 76, 189
Providence Elementary School, 13

R

Random Hill subdivision, 28
refreshment stands, 105
restaurants, 102. *See also specific restaurants*
roadside stands, 68
Robertson farm, 129
Route 50-66 Association, 41
Russell store, 133, 147–48
Rustic Glen, 140

S

Safeway grocery stores, 193
Sanitary Grocery Company, 193
sawmill businesses, 99–102, 104
school buses, 103, 113
schools, 74, 103. *See also specific schools*
sewer pumping station, 40–41
Shell gas stations, 9, 12
shopping centers, 12, 16, 33–34. *See also specific shopping centers*
Sidney Lanier School, 14

Silver Moon Restaurant, 83–84
Sisson distillery, 133–34, 145
slaughterhouses, 86
Spruce Avenue, 132
Squirrel Hill ("The Kitchen Home"), 167–68
stagecoach stops, 29
State Farm Insurance Company, 126–27
stone quarries, 79
subdivisions. *See specific subdivisions*
Summit Drive, 141
swimming, 65, 160

T

taverns, 144
Ted Britt Ford, 8–9
10th Maine Volunteers, 109
Texaco gas station, 84
timber businesses, 112
tollgate on Warrenton Pike, 86
tollhouse for Little River Turnpike, 67
tourist cabins, 1, 81
transmission shops, 126–27
trees, 24, 64–65, 106–10
trolley, 159
truck farms, 31, 135
25th Maine Infantry, 107
29 Drive-In Theater, 150

U

United Bank, 9

V

Vale community, 156, 164–68
Vale Elementary School, 166–67
Vale Methodist Church, 166–67
Virginia City amusement park, 149
Virginia Department of Highways, 38, 150
Virginia Electric and Power Company, 194–95
Virginia Prison System, Camp 30, 73, 189
Virginia Public Service Company, 193

W

wagon teams, 23
Waples Mill, 174
Waples Mill area map, 6
Waples Mill community, 156
Waples Mill dam, 173
Waples Mill Elementary, 178
Waples Mill Manor subdivision, 163–64
Waples Mill millrace, 170–72, 174
Waple store, 175
Warrenton Turnpike, tollgate on, 86
Washington Farmers' Market, 42, 192
Washington Monument, 78
Wegmans grocery store, 126, 144
welfare shelter, 38
Wells Mission, 17–18
wood businesses, 112
World War II
    Adm. Gallery in, 165
    prisoner-of-war camp, 73, 76, 189
    V. Sutphin and, 193–95

Property Index

The first number listed in the column to the right of the property refers you to the map page; the second number refers you to the text page. For example: Property 9 will be found on the Jermantown Map (page 3) and this property's descriptive text will be found on pages 16 and 17.

Location 43	5, 116–18	Property 25A	5, 98	Property 54B	5, 114
Location 44	5, 118	Property 26	5, 98	Property 55	3, 36
		Property 26A	5, 98–99	Property 55A	3, 36
Property 1	8	Property 27	5, 99	Property 55B	3, 36
Property 2	3, 8	Property 28	5, 99	Property 56	3, 37
Property 3	3, 8	Property 28A	5, 99	Property 56A	3, 38
Property 4	3, 8	Property 29	5, 102	Property 57	3, 38
Property 5	3, 9	Property 30	5, 103	Property 57A	3, 38
Property 6	9–11	Property 31	5, 103	Property 58	3, 39–40
Property 7	3, 12	Property 32	5, 104	Property 58A	3, 40
Property 7A	3, 12	Property 33	5, 104	Property 59	3, 41–43
Property 7B	3, 12	Property 33A	5, 104–5	Property 60	3, 46–50
Property 8	3, 16	Property 34	5, 105	Property 60A	3, 46, 51
Property 9	3, 16–17	Property 35	5, 105	Property 60B	3, 51–52
Property 11	3, 22–25	Property 35A	5, 105–6	Property 61	3, 53–56
Property 12	3, 26–28, 31	Property 37	5, 114	Property 62	3, 57–60
Property 13	3, 28–30	Property 38	5, 114	Property 63	3, 64–65
Property 14	3, 31	Property 39	5, 115	Property 64	3, 26, 31, 64–65, 67
Property 15	3, 31	Property 40	5, 115	Property 65	3, 66–67
Property 16	3, 32–33	Property 41	5, 115	Property 66	3, 67
Property 16A	3, 33	Property 42	5, 115–16	Property 67	3, 68
Property 17	3, 33	Property 43	5, 116–18	Property 68	5, 112
Property 18	3, 33	Property 46	5, 112–13	Property 101	3, 70
Property 19	3, 33	Property 46A	5, 118	Property 102	3, 70
Property 20	3, 34	Property 47	5, 119–20	Property 103	3, 70–71
Property 21	5, 92–94	Property 48	5, 120	Property 104	3, 71
Property 21A	5, 94	Property 49	5, 120	Property 105	3, 71
Property 22	5, 94, 96	Property 50	5, 120–21	Property 106	3, 71
Property 23	5, 93, 95–96	Property 51	5, 121	Property 107	3, 72
Property 23A	5, 97	Property 52	5, 121–23	Property 108	3, 72–73, 189
Property 24	5, 97	Property 54	5, 113	Property 108A	3, 74
Property 25	5, 97–98	Property 54A	5, 114	Property 108B	3, 74–75

Property Index

Property 108C	3, 75	Property 141	3, 83–84	Property 203A	3, 13
Property 108D	3, 75	Property 142	3, 84–85	Property 204	3, 13
Property 108E	3, 75–76	Property 143	3, 84–85	Property 205	3, 14
Property 113	4, 126, 144	Property 144	3, 85	Property 205A	3, 14
Property 114	4, 126, 144	Property 145	3, 85–86	Property 205B	3, 14
Property 115	4, 145	Property 146	3, 86	Property 206	6, 184
Property 116	4, 145	Property 146A	3, 87–89	Property 207	6, 185
Property 117	4, 145	Property 147	4, 126	Property 208	6, 185
Property 118	4, 146–48	Property 148	4, 126–28	Property 209	6, 187
Property 119	4, 147	Property 149	4, 128	Property 210	6, 186
Property 120	4, 147–48	Property 150	4, 128	Property 211	6, 186
Property 121	4, 148	Property 151	4, 128–29	Property 212	6, 186–87
Property 122	4, 148	Property 151A	4, 129	Property 213	6, 187
Property 123	4, 148–49	Property 153	4, 129–30	Property 213A	6, 188
Property 124	4, 149	Property 154	4, 130	Property 214	6, 189
Property 124A	4, 150	Property 155	4, 130	Property 215	3, 52
Property 124B	4, 150	Property 156	4, 130–31	Property 216	3, 52, 54
Property 125	4, 149–50	Property 156A	4, 131	Property 217	6, 157
Property 126	4, 150–51	Property 157	4, 131–32	Property 218	6, 157
Property 127	4, 151	Property 158	4, 132	Property 219	6, 157
Property 128	4, 151	Property 158A	4, 132	Property 220	6, 157–58
Property 128A	4, 151–52	Property 158B	4, 132	Property 221	6, 158
Property 128B	4, 152	Property 158C	4, 133	Property 222	6, 158
Property 128C	4, 153	Property 159	4, 133	Property 223	6, 158–59
Property 129	3, 78	Property 160	4, 133–34	Property 224	6, 159
Property 130	3, 78	Property 161	4, 134–35	Property 225	6, 160–61
Property 131	3, 78	Property 162	4, 135	Property 226	6, 160, 162
Property 132	3, 78	Property 163	4, 135	Property 226A	6, 162
Property 133	3, 79	Property 164	4, 135	Property 226B	6, 162–64
Property 134	3, 79	Property 165	4, 135–36	Property 227	6, 170–74
Property 135	3, 79	Property 166	4, 136	Property 228	6, 175
Property 136	3, 79	Property 166A	4, 136	Property 228A	6, 175–76
Property 137	3, 79–80	Property 166B	4, 137–39	Property 229	6, 176
Property 138	3, 80	Property 167	4, 139	Property 230	6, 176
Property 139	3, 80	Property 168	4, 139	Property 231	6, 176–77
Property 140	3, 81	Property 169	4, 140–41	Property 232	6, 177
Property 140A	3, 81	Property 170	4, 141	Property 233	6, 178
Property 140B	3, 81–82	Property 201	3, 12	Property 234	6, 178
Property 140C	3, 82–83	Property 202	3, 13	Property 235	6, 178–79
Property 140D	3, 83	Property 203	3, 13	Property 236	6, 179–82